Spelling For ADULTS

Natasha Attard Ph.D

Printed in the USA

ISBN Paperback: 978-9918-9594-0-2

DEDICATION

For my sons, Giovanni and Beppe—my greatest joy and inspiration. May you always embrace learning and chase your dreams—the world is yours to discover.

Also by Natasha Attard, Ph.D.

The Spelling Practice Workbook 6th Grade: Guided Activities to Increase your Word Power. Consolidates and Complements Homeschooling of the English Language

The Spelling Practice Workbook 7th Grade: Guided Activities to Increase your Word Power. Consolidates and Complements Homeschooling of the English Language

The Spelling Practice Workbook 8th Grade: Guided Activities to Increase your Word Power. Consolidates and Complements Homeschooling of the English Language

Vocabulary and Spelling Practice 7th Grade: Intensive Practice Workbook and Guided Activities to Increase Your Word Power.

Vocabulary Building 7th Grade Workbook: Guided Activities to Increase your Word Power. Consolidates and Complements Homeschooling of the English Language

Spelling High School Workbook Grades 9-10: Vocabulary and Writing Practice with Interactive Activities.

Spelling High School Workbook Grades 11-12: Advanced Vocabulary and Writing Practice for College Readiness

Table of Contents

A Message from the Author

If you've ever felt frustrated or even embarrassed about your spelling, you're not alone. Many adults struggle with spelling, and despite what some may say, this is not just a skill for children. In today's world, where AI and spell checkers exist at our fingertips, some might question whether learning to spell still matters. But I believe that spelling—like any other skill—is about more than just convenience.

Spelling is about confidence. It's about self-empowerment. It's about taking pride in your ability to communicate clearly and effectively. Just as people choose to improve their fitness despite having cars to drive them places, people choose to improve their spelling—not because they have to, but because they want to be better.

This book is not just a collection of rules and exercises. It's a tool to help you take control of your learning through practice and perseverance. My goal is to support you on this journey, to help you spell with confidence, and to remind you that learning is always possible—at any stage of life.

To further support you, I've created a free supplementary spelling program on my website, where you'll find additional practice activities. I encourage you to take advantage of this resource and make the most of your learning experience.

I commend you for taking this step. Stick with it, and you will see progress. Most importantly, I hope you find satisfaction in your improvement and joy in the journey.

Wishing you success,
Natasha Attard

How to Use this Book

This book is designed to help you understand, practice, and improve your spelling in a structured yet engaging way. Each unit builds on key spelling principles, providing you with the tools to recognize patterns, apply rules, and develop confidence in your writing.

The book is divided into three modules, each focusing on a different aspect of spelling and writing:

- **Module 1** covers the fundamentals of spelling, addressing common mistakes, essential rules, and foundational spelling patterns.
- **Module 2** delves into more advanced and challenging spelling rules and patterns, many of which adults commonly struggle with. These have been simplified and broken down into structured, bite-sized lessons to make learning easier and more effective.
- **Module 3** shifts the focus to written communication, helping you apply your spelling skills in practical contexts such as writing emails, résumés, reports, and other professional or everyday writing tasks.

The Lessons
The lessons in this book follow a structured but flexible approach. If you're new to spelling practice or have significant difficulties, it's best to follow the lessons in order, as each one builds upon the last. If you're already familiar with some spelling patterns but struggle in specific areas, you can jump ahead to the lessons most relevant to you. Throughout the book, you'll find plenty of space to write your answers and take notes, helping you track your learning. Tables and visual aids are included to simplify complex spelling rules, and a mix of exercises ensures that practice remains engaging and effective.

Progress Portals
At the end of each module, you'll find a Progress Portal—an online test designed to help you assess your progress. These tests focus on how well you've mastered the lessons so far and highlight areas that may need further practice. Each test is password-protected, with the passwords provided in the textbook. The goal of these assessments is to help

track your journey and ensure steady progress while identifying where to focus your efforts.

Supplementary Spelling Practice Program

To reinforce your learning, each unit has a free supplementary spelling worksheet, available for download. These printable activities provide extra practice beyond the textbook, strengthening your understanding of spelling rules and patterns. It's recommended that you print and complete them to reinforce what you've learned. Each worksheet includes an answer key for self-checking, allowing you to track your improvement. No sign-up or email submission is required to download the worksheets.

Take a Break

Some lessons and activities have been carefully designed to be as learner-friendly and structured as possible, breaking down spelling concepts into manageable steps. However, despite these efforts, some exercises may still feel challenging or intensive. When this happens, it's important to take a break. To help with this, the book provides free access to crossword puzzles and word search games—a great way to rest while still engaging with words. Like the supplementary worksheets, these resources are available online and require no sign-up to access.

Your Learning, Your Journey

This book is here to support you, not overwhelm you. Spelling is a skill that improves with practice, and every step you take brings you closer to mastering it. Work at your own pace, use the resources available, and enjoy the process. Progress happens with persistence, and you're already on your way.

Key Features of This Book

✓ Structured Lessons
✓ Targeted Practice
✓ Space for Writing and Notes
✓ Memory Aids
✓ Self-Assessment and Reflection
✓ Supplementary Worksheets
✓ Take a Break Puzzles

MODULE 1:

Essential Spelling Rules and Patterns

- **Unit 1: Commonly Confused Everyday Words**
  - **Lesson 1:** *You're, Your*
  - **Lesson 2:** *Its, It's*
  - **Lesson 3:** *They're, Their, There*
  - **Lesson 4:** *Than, Then*
  - **Lesson 5:** *Where, Were, Wear, We're*
  - **Lesson 6:** *To, Too, Two*
  - **Lesson 7:** *Buy, By, Bye*
  - **Lesson 8:** *Hear, Here*
  - **Lesson 9:** *Of, Off*
  - **Lesson 10:** *Right, Write*

- **Unit 2: Plural Suffixes and Their Rules**
  - **Lesson 11: Plural Suffixes** *-s* **and** *-es*
  - **Lesson 12: The Plural Suffixes of Nouns ending in** *-is*
  - **Lesson 13: The Plural Suffixes** *-ies* **and** *-ves*

- **Unit 3: Spelling Complex Words in Syllables**
  - **Lesson 14: Sounding Out Syllables**

- **Progress Portal 1: Reflect and Assess -** *A checkpoint to review and assess your progress, providing an opportunity for self-reflection and additional practice on challenging areas.*

SPELLING FOR ADULTS ©2025

Unit 1: Commonly Confused Everyday Words

Introduction

Many words in English sound alike yet have different meanings and spellings. These words, known as homophones, can be especially tricky when writing. I understand that even basic words can sometimes be challenging, and it's perfectly normal to feel frustrated when errors occur. This unit comprises ten concise lessons that focus on the basic homophones encountered in everyday writing—such as *your* versus *you're*, *its* versus *it's*, and *there* versus *their*. Although they may seem simple, these words are among the most commonly confused in English, and many adults struggle with using them correctly.

Through targeted practice and by developing your own mnemonic strategies, you will gain a clear understanding of each homophone's meaning and usage. This approach will strengthen your retention and help ensure that you use these essential words correctly in your writing.

Unit Overview

Each lesson in this unit introduces two or three sets of homophones and provides:

- **Definitions:** Concise explanations of each word's meaning.
- **Examples:** Sentences that illustrate proper usage.
- **Memory Aids:** Mnemonic devices (indicated by the lightbulb icon) to enhance your recall.
- **Exercises:** Writing tasks designed to reinforce learning.

How to Use This Unit

Begin by assessing your familiarity with these homophones—identify those you are confident with and those that tend to confuse you. While you may choose to skip the ones you know well, reviewing them can further reinforce your skills. Then, follow these steps:

Step 1: Work through each lesson's definitions, examples, and memory aids before completing the exercises. This approach will deepen your understanding and retention by encouraging you to:

- **Reflect Critically:** Answer guided prompts to enhance your understanding.
- **Personalize Your Learning:** Develop your own mental associations to remember each word's spelling and usage.
- **Engage in Practice:** Complete varied writing activities to consolidate your skills.

Step 2: After finishing the lessons, download the supplementary worksheet from the online Supplementary Practice Program. This worksheet is specifically designed to reinforce the content of this unit through targeted activities. The QR code and download link are provided at the end of the unit, following Lesson 10.

These steps are designed to build your confidence, improve recall, and enhance your ability to use homophones correctly in everyday contexts.

By the end of this unit, you will be able to:
- **Confidently differentiate between basic homophones in your writing.**
- **Apply these homophones accurately to ensure clear and effective communication.**
- **Develop and use personalized mnemonic strategies to remember correct usage.**

You're

- Contraction of *you are*.
- Example: **You're** going to love this!
- Use when you can replace it with *you are* and the sentence still makes sense.

Your

- Indicates **possession**.
- Example: Is this **your** book?
- Use when referring to **something that belongs to someone.**

 I remember "you're" is two words (you are) because of the apostrophe. Whenever I see "your," I think "your things" to remind myself it shows ownership.

 When should you use "**you're**," and how is it different from "**your**"?
Use your own words as much as possible to explain.

 Create a **memory aid**, to remember the difference.

Activity 1: Fill in the blank with either *your* or *you're* to complete each sentence correctly.

1. Let me know when __*You're*__ ready to discuss your next project.

2. Don't forget to bring __*your*__ ID badge to work tomorrow.

3. Please double-check __*your*__ email for any spelling mistakes before sending it.

4. I can tell __*You're*__ really committed to improving your skills.

5. __*You're*__ welcome to join us for lunch if you have time.

6. I think __*your*__ lunch is in the fridge, right next to mine.

7. __*Your*__ appointment with the manager is scheduled for 3 p.m.

8. If __*you're*__ planning to take a vacation, be sure to submit your request early.

9. __*You're*__ doing a great job with those customer orders—keep it up!

10. Remember to lock __*your*__ car before coming inside.

11. Whether __*you're*__ exploring a new city or revisiting old memories, travel always broadens __*your*__ perspective.

12. Trust in __*your*__ abilities, even when __*you're*__ unsure of the outcome.

13. Whether __*you're*__ meeting new people or deepening connections, __*your*__ communication skills are key.

14. When __*you're*__ facing new challenges, remember that __*your*__ resilience is one of your greatest assets.

15. __*Your*__ determination shows, even when __*you're*__ faced with setbacks.

Its	• Possessive form of *it*. • Example: The cat licked **its** paws. • Use when saying that something **belongs to it**.

It's	• Contraction of *it is* or *it has*. • Example (It has): **It's** been a very long time since I had cotton candy! • Example (It is): **It's** unacceptable that we have to wait for one month for an appointment with the cardiologist! • Use when you can replace it with *it is/has* and the sentence still makes sense.

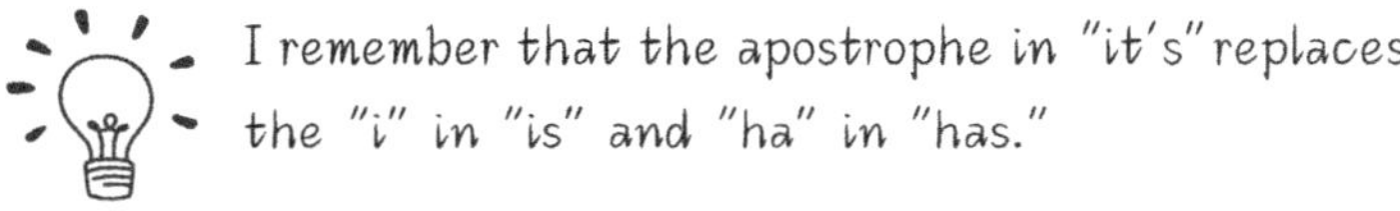

 When should you use "<u>**its**</u>," and how is it different from "<u>**it's**</u>"? *Use your own words as much as possible to explain.*	 **My Memory Aid**

 # Activity 2: Fill in the blank with either *its* or *it's* to complete each sentence correctly.

1. The company is proud of ________________ commitment to reducing waste and improving sustainability.

2. The tree lost many of ________________ leaves during the strong winds last night.

3. The microwave keeps beeping to let me know ________________ done heating up my lunch.

4. A cat uses ________________ tail to help maintain balance when climbing.

5. The carwash is busy today, but ________________ worth the wait to get a spotless vehicle.

6. ________________ been a long day, so I think I'll relax with a cup of tea when I get home.

7. The smartphone has a crack on ________________ screen, so I'll need to get it repaired.

8. The restaurant is known for ________________ cozy atmosphere and friendly service.

9. ________________ a good idea to check your grocery list before heading to the supermarket.

10. At the coffee shop, ________________ best to order early to avoid the morning rush.

11. The dog chased ________________ tail for hours, never seeming to get tired.

12. ________________ been a long time since we last had a family gathering.

13. ________________ small size makes the hummingbird one of the most fascinating creatures in the animal kingdom.

          SPELLING FOR ADULTS ©2025

They're

- Contraction of *they are.*
- The **apostrophe** combines *they* and *are* into one word.

Their

- Possessive form of *they.*
- Example: **Their** car is new.
- Use when saying that something **belongs to them.**

There

- Refers to a **place or existence** (adverb of place).
- Use when indicating **a place or presence**.
- **Place:** The book is over **there**.
- **Existence: There are** over 530 species of sharks in our oceans.

"They're" has an apostrophe because it combines "they" and "are."

"Their" contains "heir," which reminds me it's about something that belongs to them, like an inheritance.

"There" contains "here," helping me remember it refers to a place.

 When should you use "**they're**," "**their**," and "**there**," and how are they different from each other?
Use your own words as much as possible to explain.

 My Memory Aid

 **Activity 3: Fill in the blank with either _they're, their,_ or _there,_ to complete each sentence correctly.**

1. During the Renaissance, __________________ was a surge in art, literature, and scientific discovery.

2. The students presented __________________ research on how climate change affects local wildlife.

3. Historians study the lives of individuals to understand __________________ impact on society.

4. __________________ launching a new art exhibit downtown to celebrate local artists.

5. At the library, __________________ hosting workshops on digital skills for adults.

6. __________________ remembering loved ones who served in the military on Veterans Day.

7. In the library, __________________ are countless resources on global cultures and traditions.

8. __________________ was a significant shift in society when the internet became widely accessible.

9. Parents are concerned about __________________ children's safety on social media.

10. Artists often find inspiration in __________________ surroundings, from cityscapes to rural landscapes.

11. Since ___________________ both teachers, they often discuss educational trends and challenges.

12. If you walk down Main Street, ___________________ are several small businesses worth exploring.

13. In the library, ___________________ are countless resources on global cultures and traditions.

14. Many people take pride in ___________________ cultural heritage and celebrate it through festivals.

15. ___________________ is a museum in town that showcases the history of the early settlers.

Need a break? *Head over to the Take a Break page for free fun crossword and word search puzzles created just for you. Scan the QR code or visit the link below to get started!*

https://natashascripts.com/takeabreak-spelling-puzzles/

<table>
<tr><td>

Than

</td><td>

- Used for **comparisons**.
- Example: She is tall**er than** him.
- *Than* has an *a* like *compare*.

</td></tr>
</table>

<table>
<tr><td>

Then

</td><td>

- Refers to **time** or **sequence**.
- Example: Finish work, **then** relax.
- Use when discussing **time** or **order**.
- *Then* has an *e* like *time*.

</td></tr>
</table>

I remember the difference between "than" and "then" because "th<u>a</u>n" is used to compare, and comp<u>a</u>re has an "a," while "th<u>e</u>n" is connected with tim<u>e</u>, and tim<u>e</u> has an "e."

<table>
<tr><td>

When should you use "**<u>than</u>**," and how is it different from "**<u>then</u>**"?
Use your own words as much as possible to explain.

</td><td>

My Memory Aid

</td></tr>
</table>

 **Activity 4: Use the context in each paragraph to decide if *than* or *then* fits best, and write your choice in each blank.**

1. Studies show that individuals who engage in active learning retain information better _____________________ those who passively read or listen. This is why techniques like summarizing, questioning, and self-testing are encouraged, as they involve deeper cognitive processing than simple memorization.

2. In statistical analysis, larger sample sizes generally provide more accurate results _____________________ smaller ones. With more data points, researchers can reduce the margin of error and increase the reliability of their findings.

3. In a controlled experiment, scientists observe and record data to test a hypothesis. First, they set up the experiment by identifying variables and constants. _______________, they run multiple trials, carefully noting results. Afterward, they analyze the data to see if it supports or disproves their original hypothesis.

4. Some areas receive significantly more rainfall _____________________ others, leading to diverse ecosystems around the world. For example, rainforests experience high levels of precipitation, creating lush environments, whereas deserts receive less rain, resulting in arid landscapes with specialized plant and animal life.

5. In many novels, the climax represents a turning point for the protagonist. The character might face a dilemma or make a crucial decision. ____________________, in the resolution, the consequences of that decision are revealed, bringing the story to a conclusion and leaving readers with a lasting impression.

6. The Impressionist movement began with a small group of artists who challenged traditional painting techniques. ____________________, as their work gained recognition, more artists adopted the style, leading to broader acceptance of Impressionism.

7. In physics, it's often said that actions have consequences. For instance, friction is stronger on rough surfaces ____________________ on smooth ones, causing more resistance to motion.

8. In the animal kingdom, some species are more adaptable to changing environments ____________________ others. Animals with greater genetic diversity often have a better chance of surviving in fluctuating conditions. This adaptability explains why certain species thrive in various habitats while others are confined to specific regions.

9. The Industrial Revolution marked a period of intense change in production and technology. Before this era, most manufacturing was done by hand. _____________________, with the invention of machinery, factory production soared, leading to a rapid expansion of cities as people moved closer to factories for work.

10. To solve a complex equation, you begin by isolating one variable. _____________________, you simplify each term step-by-step until you reach a solution. Once the solution is found, it's important to double-check each step to ensure the calculations were correct.

Lesson 5: *Where, Were, Wear, We're*

Where

- An adverb, referring to a **place**.
- Example: **Where** are you?
- Use when asking about or referring to a **location**.

Were

- A verb, past tense of *are*.
- Example: They **were** happy.
- Use when talking about something in the **past**.

Wear

- A verb, meaning **to put on clothing or accessories**.
- Example: She's **wearing** her new coat.

We're

- A contraction of *we are*.
- Example: **We're** excited to join.
- Use *we're* when *we are* fits in the sentence.

 It helps me to remember that "<u>where</u>" contains "<u>here</u>," linking it to a place. "Wear" takes "<u>ing</u>" because you're wear<u>ing</u> clothes, while "where" and "were" don't get dressed. Also, the apostrophe in "we're" replaces the "<u>a</u>" in "are."

When should you use "**<u>where</u>**" and "**<u>were</u>**," and how are they different from each other?
Use your own words as much as possible to explain.

When should you use "**<u>wear</u>**"?

What does "**<u>we're</u>**" mean, and when should you use it?

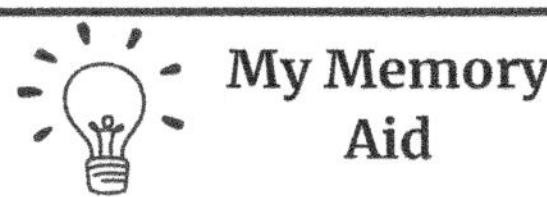 My Memory Aid

 **Activity 5: Use the context in each sentence to determine whether *where*, *were*, *wear*, or *we're* fits best. Write your choice in the blank.**

1. In medieval times, knights would _____________________ heavy armor to protect themselves in battle.

2. True peace is often found _____________________ silence meets the soul.

3. The tools _____________________ scattered across the workbench, ready for the next repair.

4. Doctors and nurses _____________________ scrubs to maintain hygiene and comfort during their shifts.

5. _____________________ determined to finish the project on time, despite the setbacks.

6. Communities thrive _____________________ people feel safe and supported.

7. The café _____________________ we had breakfast had the best view of the mountains.

8. We _____________________ discussing next quarter's goals when the fire alarm went off.

9. The vegetables _____________________ overcooked, but the sauce saved the dish.

10. _____________________ lucky to live in an era where technology connects us so easily.

11. Legends say that warriors would _____________________ talismans to protect them from evil spirits.

12. He prefers to _____________________ casual clothes, even when attending formal events.

13. The workers _____________________ trained on the new assembly line procedures last week.

14. _____________________ the road forks, you'll find a hidden trail leading to the beach.

15. I'll show you _____________________ I found the recipe for this delicious cake.

16. While hiking up the trail, _____________________ hoping to catch a glimpse of the sunrise.

17. _____________________ planning a surprise birthday party, so don't let the secret slip!

18. Customers _____________________ lining up outside the store for the grand opening.

19. In traditional Japanese culture, women _____________________ kimonos during formal ceremonies.

20. In the kitchen, _____________________ experimenting with new spices to create a unique dish.

To

- A preposition indicating **direction** or **connection**.
- Example: I'm going **to** the store.
- Use for **movement**, **direction**, or **connecting ideas**.

Too

- An adverb, meaning *also*, indicating **inclusion**. It also means *excessively*.
- Example: She works **too** hard but she wants to relax **too**.
- Use to mean *also* or to describe an *excessive degree*.

Two

- A noun or adjective indicating the **number 2**.
- Example: I asked for **two** donuts, but I got twelve - talk about a sweet misunderstanding!

To remember the difference between "to" and "too," I note that the <u>extra</u> "<u>o</u>" in "too" indicates <u>excess</u>. To remember which word represents the number 2, I think of the word "t<u>w</u>ins," which also has a "<u>w</u>," just like "t<u>w</u>o."

What does "<u>to</u>" mean, and how is it used in a sentence? Write one example to show its meaning. *Use your own words as much as possible to explain.*

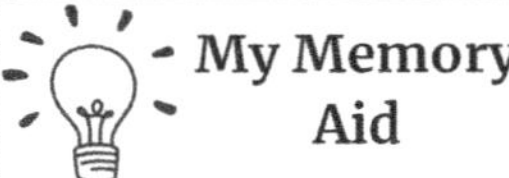
My Memory Aid

What does "<u>too</u>" mean, and how is it different from "<u>to</u>"?

What's the easiest way to remember that "<u>two</u>" is not the same as "<u>to</u>" or "<u>too</u>"?

 **Activity 6: Use the context in each sentence to determine whether *to*, *too*, or *two* fits best. Write your choice in the blank.**

1. It took me ______________ tries ______________ parallel park, but in my defense, the space was tiny.

2. The spicy curry was delicious, but it was way ______________ hot for my taste buds ______________ handle!

3. I went ______________ the gym this morning... only ______________ sit in the café and drink coffee.

4. She went ______________ the store ______________ buy milk but came back with a new coffee machine instead.

5. The kids tried ______________ sneak ______________ the fridge at midnight, but the squeaky door gave them away.

6. She said she'd bring snacks ______________ the party ______________, but all she brought was a bag of ice.

7. He works ______________ hard during the week and then naps ______________ much on the weekends.

8. She brought ______________ cakes ______________ the office party – one to share and one ______________ hide in her desk.

9. I set my alarm ______________ hours early, but somehow, I was still late for work.

10. I drove to the meeting an hour early, only ______________ realize it was scheduled for tomorrow.

11. He wanted ______________ ask for a raise, but his nerves got the best of him— so he asked for a stapler instead.

     SPELLING FOR ADULTS ©2025

12. I wanted _____________ join the dance class _____________, but my two left feet had other plans.

13. The puppy was _____________ cute _____________ resist, so now I'm a proud dog mom of three.

14. I asked for _____________ sugars in my coffee, and the barista handed me _____________ cookies instead.

15. The magician said he had _____________ tricks up his sleeve, but all I saw was a rabbit and a pigeon.

Buy

- A verb, meaning *to purchase something*.
- Example: I want to **buy** a car.

By

- A preposition indicating **location** or **method**.
- Example (Location): She sat **by the window**, enjoying the view of the rain outside.
- Example (Method): He completed the entire project **by using** only free online resources.
- Use for **proximity** or **means of doing something**.

Bye

- Short for *goodbye.*
- Example: Say **bye** to your friends.
- Use when **leaving** or **saying farewell**.

I remember that "buy" means "purchase" because both words contain the letter "u." To remember the difference between "by" and "bye," I think of "by<u>e</u>" containing an "<u>e</u>," just like in "far<u>e</u>well," which reminds me it's used to say good<u>bye</u>.

 Write a sentence using "**<u>by</u>**" to describe something located **near or next to** something else.

In your own words, explain how "**<u>bye</u>**" and "**<u>buy</u>**" are different in meaning and use.

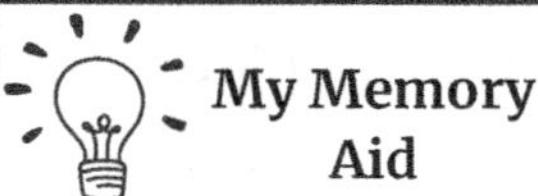 **My Memory Aid**

 **Activity 7: Use the context in each sentence to determine whether *by*, *bye*, or *buy* fits best. Write your choice in the blank.**

1. She walked ______________ the shop, tempted to ______________ the dress in the window, but instead whispered ______________ to her reflection.

2. The library is located right ______________ the main square in town.

3. The parcel was delivered ______________ courier within two days.

4. If you ______________ three books, you get a discount on the fourth one.

5. She waved ______________ to her friends as the train pulled out of the station.

6. "______________ for now!" she said, promising to call later that evening.

7. I stopped ______________ the bakery to ______________ a loaf of bread and said ______________ to the friendly cashier.

8. He saved enough money to finally ______________ his dream car.

9. There's a beautiful café ______________ the lake where you can enjoy the view.

10. "Say ______________ to Grandma before we leave," Mom reminded her kids.

11. The little girl cheerfully said ______________ to her teacher on the last day of school.

12. I need to ______________ some groceries before the store closes.

13. He completed the project ______________ working late every night.

14. On my way ______________ the park, I decided to ______________ an ice cream and waved ______________ to a friend.

15. You can ______________ tickets online or swing ______________ the box office to pick them up in person.

16. "I'll stop ______________ your house tomorrow to say ______________ before my trip," he promised.

17. She said ______________ to her friends as they walked ______________ the coffee shop.

18. They hurried ______________ the ticket counter to ______________ their passes and whispered a quick ______________ to the attendant.

Hear

- A verb meaning *to perceive sound.*
- Example: Can you **hear** me?
- Use when talking about sound and **the sense of hearing.**

Here

- An adverb referring to **location.**
- Example: Please sit **here** while you wait for the appointment.
- Use when talking about a **place.**

 It helps me remember that "h<u>ear</u>" is about sound because it contains the word "<u>ear</u>," making it different from "here," which refers to a location.

 When should you use "**<u>hear</u>**" and "**<u>here</u>**," and how are they different from each other?
Use your own words as much as possible to explain.

 **My Memory Aid**

Activity 8: Fill in the blank with either *hear* or *here* to complete each sentence correctly.

1. It's nice to finally be _______________ after such a long journey.

2. Stand _______________ for a moment, and I'll be back with the paperwork.

3. I can't believe it's already been a year since we moved _______________.

4. You should _______________ the advice of those who have more experience in this field.

5. I often _______________ my favorite song playing in my head, even when there's no music around.

6. The instructions say to click _______________ to complete your registration.

7. He strained to _______________ what the speaker was saying over the chatter in the crowd.

8. It's so quiet in this library that you can _______________ a pin drop.

9. Please place your bags _______________ by the door so we can keep the area clear.

10. It's great to see everyone gathered _______________ for the family reunion.

11. She loves to _______________ the sound of waves crashing on the shore during her morning walks.

12. I could _______________ the birds chirping outside my window as the sun rose.

13. The best coffee shop in town is right _______________ on this corner.

14. I can't wait to _______________ your thoughts on the new book I recommended.

15. Did you _______________ the thunder last night during the storm?

16. Let's sit _______________ and enjoy the sunset together.

17. _______________ in the park, you can often _______________ the cheerful laughter of children playing.

18. I love it _______________ by the ocean because I can _______________ the soothing sound of the waves.

Of

- A preposition indicating a relationship, typically **possession** or **inclusion**.
- Example (Possession): The cover **of** the book.
- Example (Inclusion): She bought a box **of** chocolates to share with her friends.
- Use when describing **possession, a part of something, or a relationship between things.**

Off

- Indicates **movement away**, **separation**, or **disconnection.**
- Example (Movement Away): The cat jumped **off** the table.
- Example (Separation): She carefully peeled **off** the sticker from the envelope.
- Example (Disconnection): Please turn **off** the lights before leaving the room.
- Use when referring to **detaching, removing,** or **going away from something**.

 "Of" rhymes with "love," which helps me remember it's used to show connection or inclusion. The double "f" in "off" reminds me of "falling off" or "moving away," emphasizing separation.

<u>Important</u>: A common error is writing "would of" instead of "<u>would have</u>."

Remember, "would've" (not "would of") is short for "would have."

 Write two sentences using **"<u>of</u>"** to indicate: (i) possession, and (ii) inclusion.

In your own words, explain how **"<u>of</u>"** and **"<u>off</u>"** are different in meaning and use.

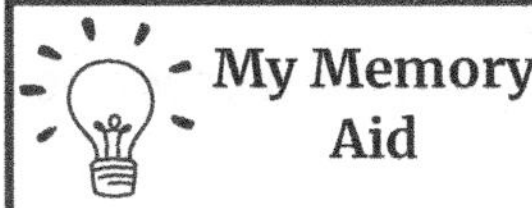 **My Memory Aid**

SPELLING FOR ADULTS ©2025

Activity 9: Use the context in each sentence to determine whether *of* or *off* fits best. Write your choice in the blank.

1. The color ___________ the sky changed as the sun set.

2. She was proud ___________ her accomplishments.

3. The bird flew ___________ the branch when it heard a noise.

4. She carefully took her coat ___________ before hanging it up.

5. The book ___________ poems was a bestseller.

6. The alarm clock went ___________ at exactly 6 a.m.

7. The scent ___________ fresh flowers filled the room.

8. He jumped ___________ the diving board into the pool.

9. Please wipe the dust ___________ the shelf before arranging the books.

10. He's a man ___________ great wisdom and kindness.

11. The idea ___________ traveling to Europe excites her.

12. The sale offers 20% ___________ all electronics this weekend.

13. Turn the television ___________ if no one is watching.

14. A piece ___________ cake would be perfect for dessert.

15. The crown ___________ the king was adorned with precious jewels.

16. The power went ___________ during the thunderstorm.

17. The aroma ___________ freshly baked bread filled the kitchen.

18. A bouquet ___________ roses was placed on the dining table.

19. He brushed ___________ the crumbs from his shirt after lunch.

20. The car sped ___________ as soon as the traffic light turned green.

Right

- An adjective meaning **correct**, or
- a noun/adverb referring to the direction **opposite of left**.
- Example (Correct): You were absolutely **right** about the outcome of the meeting.
- Example (Noun – Opposite of Left): Take a **right** at the next intersection to reach the museum.
- Use when referring to **accuracy**, **justice**, or the **direction opposite of left**.

Write

- A verb meaning to **create text or letters**, typically on paper or a digital device
- Example: **Write** her a letter to express our condolences.
- Use when referring to **the act of putting words down in written form**.

 "Write" has a "w," like "words," which helps me remember it's about creating text. The "ight" in "right" reminds me of "fight," making it easy to recall that when I'm right, I stand up for it.

 When should you use "**right**" and "**write**," and how are they different from each other?
Use your own words as much as possible to explain.

My Memory Aid

Activity 10: Use the context in each sentence to determine whether *right* or *write* fits best. Write your choice in the blank.

1. Can you _________________ a brief summary of the book for the class?

2. You were absolutely _________________ about the movie being fantastic!

3. Turn _________________ at the next stoplight, and you'll see the bookshop.

4. It's important to do the _________________ thing, even when no one is watching.

5. He likes to _________________ poetry in his free time to relax.

6. She decided to _________________ her memoirs as a gift for her grandchildren.

7. She has every _________________ to express her opinion during the discussion.

8. The repairman fixed the issue and got the machine working _________________ again.

9. If you don't _________________ regularly, your handwriting may become less legible.

10. He stood up for what he believed was _________________.

11. During the meeting, I was asked to _________________ the minutes for everyone.

12. The beach is just a short walk to the _________________ of the hotel entrance.

13. After the argument, she called to make things _________________ with her friend.

14. If you ___________________ down your goals, you're more likely to achieve them.

15. He asked me to ___________________ a recommendation letter for his job application.

16. I checked the map twice, and we're heading in the ___________________ direction.

17. The ___________________ tool for the job can make all the difference in how quickly it's done.

18. You should ___________________ a thank-you note to show your appreciation.

19. They hired a journalist to ___________________ an article about the upcoming event.

20. She plans to ___________________ a novel about her travels around the world.

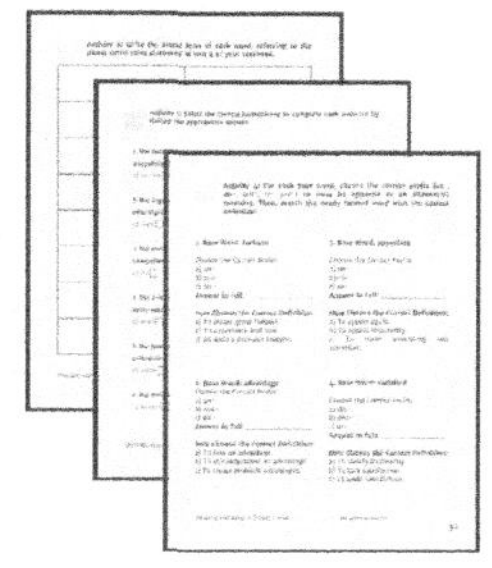

     SPELLING FOR ADULTS ©2025

Unit 2: The Essentials of Plural Spelling

Introduction
This unit focuses on plural forms—a fundamental part of English spelling and communication. A plural is the form of a noun that indicates more than one, and the most common way to form plurals in English is by adding the suffix -*s* to the end of a noun. For example, *papers*, *screens*, and *texts*.

While the -*s* suffix is the most frequently used, there are three additional plural suffixes that play a significant role in English spelling and writing. Together, these four suffixes form the foundation for plural spelling in the language. They are essential for everything from casual writing to academic and professional communication.

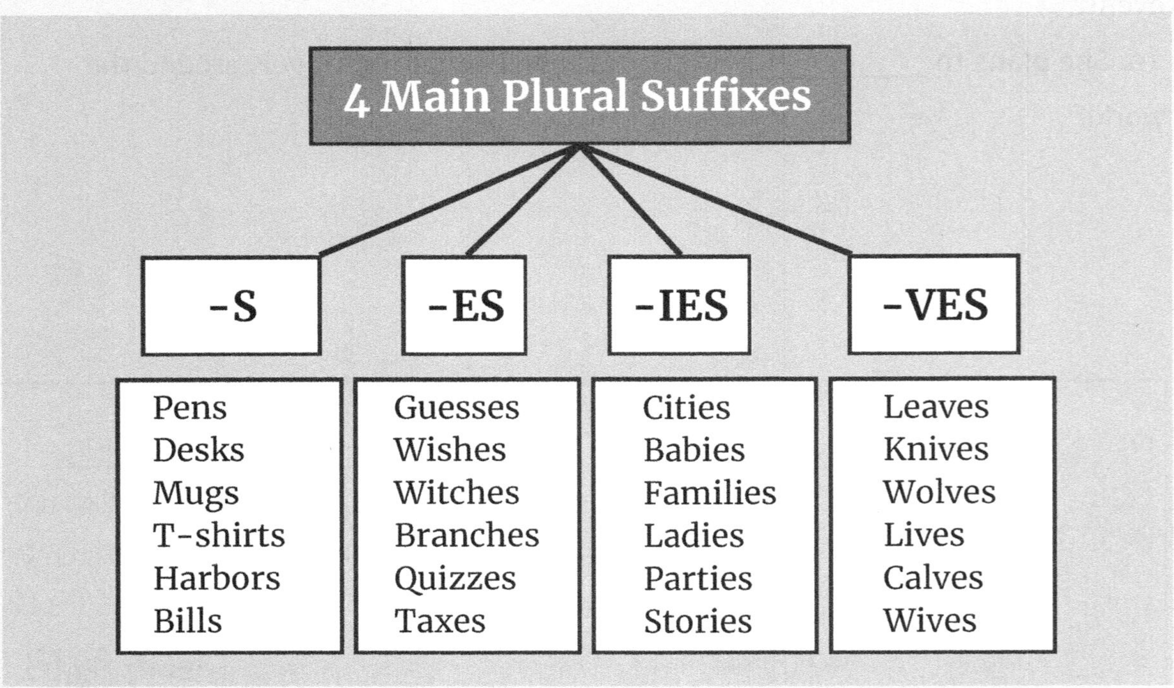

Unit Overview
The lessons in this unit include clear tables that summarize each rule for plural formation, along with examples to aid understanding and memory retention. Once you've studied these, you'll complete written activities in the subsequent lessons, designed to reinforce the rules and internalize the patterns. These activities will help ensure you can confidently apply plural spelling in your writing.

The aim of this unit is to provide clear and easy-to-follow spelling rules for forming plurals. By the end of this unit, you will:
1. **Understand the four main plural suffixes and when to use each.**
2. **Accurately apply these rules to a variety of noun endings.**
3. **Build confidence in your ability to spell plurals correctly in different contexts.**

Supplementary Practice Program
To further reinforce the lessons in this unit, you can download the corresponding supplementary worksheets designed for extra practice. The link and QR code to access these worksheets are provided at the end of this unit.

The suffix -*s* is the most commonly used plural form in the English language. To determine whether a noun takes -*s* to form its plural, it is important to be familiar with the other plural suffixes: -*es*, -*ies*, and -*ves.* These suffixes are mutually exclusive, meaning a noun that does not form its plural with -*es*, -*ies*, or -*ves* generally takes -*s*.

Here are three general rules for when a noun forms its plural with -*s*:
1. **When the noun ends in a consonant**:
   - Examples: Ca**b**s, sa**c**s, be**d**s, roo**f**s, bags.
2. **When the noun ends in a vowel followed by** *y*:
   - Example: K**ey** → keys.
3. **When the noun ends with** *ff*:
   - Example: Cli**ff** → cliffs

<table>
<tr><td colspan="3" align="center">-S</td></tr>
<tr><td>Add -s to most nouns that end with a consonant.</td><td>Add -s to most nouns that end with a vowel + y.</td><td>Add -s to nouns that end in -ff.</td></tr>
<tr><td>Car<u>d</u> → Cards
Chai<u>r</u> → Chairs
Cloc<u>k</u> → Clocks
Des<u>k</u> → Desks
Fac<u>t</u> → Facts
Lam<u>p</u> → Lamps
Plan<u>t</u> → Plants</td><td>B<u>oy</u> → Boys
Journ<u>ey</u> → Journeys
Monk<u>ey</u> → Monkeys
Pl<u>ay</u> → Plays
T<u>oy</u> → Toys
Vall<u>ey</u> → Valleys</td><td>Bluff → Bluffs
Chaff → Chaffs
Cliff → Cliffs
Scoff → Scoffs
Sniff → Sniffs
Stuff → Stuffs
Whiff → Whiffs</td></tr>
</table>

-ES

The suffix *-es* is added to nouns under the following conditions:

1. **Nouns ending with a silent *-e*.**
   - Examples: Ax<u>e</u> → axes, ros<u>e</u> → roses.
2. **Nouns ending with hissing sounds like *-ss*, *-x*, and *-z*.**
   - Examples: Dre<u>ss</u> → dresses, bo<u>x</u> → boxes, bu<u>zz</u> → buzzes.
3. **Nouns ending with swishing sounds like *-sh*, and *-ch*.**
   - Examples: Bru<u>sh</u> → brushes, ben<u>ch</u> → benches.
4. **Nouns ending in *-is*.**
   - Examples: Thes<u>is</u> → theses, bas<u>is</u> → bases.

When applying **rules 2 and 3**, it is essential to focus on the sounds of the endings, not just the letters. If the ending letters do not produce a hissing or swishing sound, the *-es* rule will not apply. For example, the word *stomach* ends in *ch*, but since it is pronounced as a hard *k* sound, the plural form is *stomachs*, not *stomaches*.

Ending with Silent *-e*	The Hissing Trio	The Swishing Duo
Add *-es* to most nouns that end in a silent *-e*.	Add *-es* to nouns ending in the hissing sounds *-ss*, *-z*, and *-x*.	Add *-es* to nouns ending in the swishing sounds *-sh* and *-ch*.
Ag<u>e</u> → Ages Ax<u>e</u> → Axes Charg<u>e</u> → Charges Pag<u>e</u> → Pages Phas<u>e</u> → Phases Plac<u>e</u> → Places Rang<u>e</u> → Ranges Siz<u>e</u> → Sizes	Dre<u>ss</u> → Dresses Hi<u>ss</u> → Hisses Fo<u>x</u> → Foxes Ta<u>x</u> → Taxes Bu<u>zz</u> → Buzzes Qui<u>z</u> → Quizzes* Addre<u>ss</u> → Addresses Cla<u>ss</u> → Classes	Bru<u>sh</u> → Brushes Chur<u>ch</u> → Churches Di<u>sh</u> → Dishes Mat<u>ch</u> → Matches Ben<u>ch</u> → Benches

* "Quiz" doubles the "z" before adding "-es" to keep its short vowel sound. This rule ensures the pronunciation remains consistent.

One of the most common mistakes in spelling plurals is using an apostrophe + s (**'s**) to form the plural of a word. This is <u>**incorrect**</u>. For example, the plural of *son* is *sons*, <u>**not**</u> *son's*.

❌ *Incorrect*	✅ Correct
The son's are happy.	The <u>sons</u> are happy.
The dog's are barking.	The <u>dogs</u> are barking.
The girl's are singing.	The <u>girls</u> are singing.

 Apostrophes are used to show **possession** or **contractions**. **They are not used to form plurals.**

Possession	Contraction
My son's birthday is tomorrow.	<u>He's</u> out at the moment. (He is)
The dog's ears are perked up.	She's been having some challenges. (She has)

Lesson 12: The Plural Suffixes of Nouns Ending in *-is*

> 💡 **Nouns ending in *-is* form their plural by replacing *-is* with *-es*.**

Common words ending in *-is*.	Less common words ending in *-is*.
• Thes**is** → Theses • Analys**is** → Analyses • Cris**is** → Crises • Emphas**is** → Emphases • Hypothes**is** → Hypotheses • Oas**is** → Oases • Bas**is** → Bases • Diagnos**is** → Diagnoses • Metamorphos**is** → Metamorphoses • Paralys**is** → Paralyses • Psychos**is** → Psychoses	• Prognos**is** → Prognoses • Parenthes**is** → Parentheses • Ax**is** → Axes • Ellips**is** → Ellipses • Synthes**is** → Syntheses • Symbios**is** → Symbioses • Necros**is** → Necroses • Seps**is** → Sepses • Arthros**is** → Arthroses

 **Activity 11: Read each statement carefully and determine whether it is true or false based on the plural rules you have learned so far.**

1. Nouns ending in a silent *-e* usually end in *-es* in the plural, e.g. *cue   cues.*

   True ☐ False ☐

2. Most nouns ending with a consonant generally form their plural by adding the suffix *-s.*

   True ☐ False ☐

SPELLING FOR ADULTS ©2025

3. Nouns ending in the hissing sounds –ss, –z, and –x usually form their plural by simply adding s.

True ☐
False ☐

4. A singular noun ending in a vowel followed by *y*, such as *donkey*, usually forms its plural by adding the suffix –s.

True ☐
False ☐

5. The swishing sounds in singular nouns are those ending in –sh or –ch.

True ☐
False ☐

6. Most nouns ending in –is, such as *analysis*, form their plural by replacing the suffix with –es.

True ☐
False ☐

7. The plural of *monkey* is *monkies*.

True ☐
False ☐

8. Most nouns ending in –ff form their plural by adding the suffix –es, as in *cliff   cliffes*.

True ☐
False ☐

9. Nouns such as *bench*, *class*, and *box* form their plurals by adding the suffix –es.

True ☐
False ☐

10. The plural of *roof* is *rooves*.

True ☐
False ☐

11. *Thesis*, *basis*, and *emphasis*, change to *theses*, *bases*, and *emphases*, in their plural forms. True ☐ False ☐

12. *Axe* becomes *axes* in its plural form, whereas *axis* also becomes *axes* in its plural form (different meaning). True ☐ False ☐

13. *Chair* becomes *chaires*, while *church* becomes *churchs* in their plural forms. True ☐ False ☐

14. *Dress* becomes *dresses*, while *address* becomes *addresses* in their plural forms. True ☐ False ☐

15. *Match* becomes *matches*, while *stomach* becomes *stomachs* in their plural form. True ☐ False ☐

Need a break? Head over to the Take a Break page for free fun crossword and word search puzzles created just for you. Scan the QR code or visit the link below to get started!

https://natashascripts.com/takeabreak-spelling-puzzles/

Lesson 13: The Plural Suffixes *-ies* and *-ves*

The suffix *-ies* is added to nouns under the following conditions:

1. Nouns ending with a **consonant followed by** *y* typically form their plural by replacing the *y* with *-ies*.

   ○ Examples: Bo<u>dy</u> → bo**dies**, memo<u>ry</u> → memo**ries**.

Note: Although this lesson focuses on plural forms of nouns, it's worth noting that verbs (action words) and adjectives (descriptive words) ending in a consonant + y often follow the same rule when conjugated or modified.

-IES

Add *-ies* **to most nouns that end in a consonant + y.**

Po<u>ny</u> → Ponies	Batte<u>ry</u> → Batteries
Ene<u>my</u> → Enemies	Compa<u>ny</u> → Companies
Colo<u>ny</u> → Colonies	Melo<u>dy</u> → Melodies
Facto<u>ry</u> → Factories	Prope<u>rty</u> → Properties
Libra<u>ry</u> → Libraries	Hob<u>by</u> → Hobbies

Singular	Plural	Example	Singular	Plural	Example
b + y	b + ies	Hob**bies**	m + y	m + ies	Mum**mies**
c + y	c + ies	Democra**cies**	n + y	n + ies	Compa**nies**
d + y	d + ies	Come**dies**	p + y	p + ies	Co**pies**
f + y*	f + ies	Uni**fies***	r + y	r + ies	F**ries**
g + y	g + ies	Aller**gies**	s + y	s + ies	Fanta**sies**
k + y**	k + ies	S**kies****	t + y	t + ies	Par**ties**
l + y	l + ies	Lil**lies**	v + y	v + ies	Na**vies**

*A significant number of words ending in "–fy" are verbs rather than nouns. However, the rule also applies to verbs, as in: "justify → justifies," "identify → identifies," and "notify → notifies."
**Nouns ending in "–ky" are rare in English. Most words with this ending are adjectives and, as such, do not take the plural form, e.g., "lucky," "rocky," and "risky."

Plural Suffix –VES

We previously noted that words ending in consonants typically take the suffix –s to form their plural. However, nouns ending in –f can be an exception to this rule. Some nouns ending in f form their plural with –s, while others use –ves.

For example:
- *Belief* becomes *beliefs* in its plural form.
- *Leaf* becomes *leaves*.

Some other nouns ending in –fe will either take the plural suffix –s or –ves.

For example:
- *Giraffe* becomes *giraffes* and *chafe* becomes *chafes*.
- *Knife* becomes *knives* and *life* becomes *lives*.

A few other nouns ending in *-f* can take either *-s* or *-ves* as acceptable plural forms. Examples include:

- Dwar**f** → dwarf**s** or dwar**ves**.
- Hoo**f** → hoof**s** or hoo**ves**.
- Scar**f** → scarf**s** or scar**ves**.
- Whar**f** → wharf**s** or whar**ves**.

Unfortunately, **there is no clear rule** to explain why certain nouns follow one pattern and not the other. Thankfully, only a small number of nouns ending in *-f* require this distinction, making them relatively easy to learn. These specific nouns are included in the tables that follow. Be sure to study them closely and work through the accompanying activities to reinforce their spelling.

-VES

Nouns ending in *-f* that form their plural with *-ves*.
Cal**f** → Calves   Shel**f** → Shelves Hal**f** → Halves   Snif**f** → Sniffs Lea**f** → Leaves   Thie**f** → Thieves Loa**f** → Loaves   Wol**f** → Wolves Shea**f** → Sheaves

<table>
<tr><td align="center">Nouns ending in -fe that form
their plural with -ves.</td></tr>
</table>

Li**fe** → Lives
Kni**fe** → Knives
Wi**fe** → Wives

<table>
<tr><td align="center">Nouns ending in -f that form their plural with -s</td></tr>
</table>

Belie**f** → Beliefs
Chie**f** → Chiefs
Handkerchie**f** → Handkerchiefs
Muf**f** → Muffs

Ree**f** → Reefs
Roo**f** → Roofs
Snif**f** → Sniffs

Activity 12: Write the correct plural form of each word in the table below.

Singular Noun	Plural Form -s -es -ies -ves	Singular Noun	Plural Form -s -es -ies -ves
Administrator		Brush	
Sale		Family	
Bench		Knife	
Cashier		Self	
Calf		Copy	
Factory		Task	
Nurse		Service	
Life		Electrician	
Enemy		Plumber	

Singular Noun	Plural Form -s -es -ies -ves	Singular Noun	Plural Form -s -es -ies -ves
Dish		Watch	
Class		Buzz	
Tax		Order	
Supply		Box	
Drawer		Store	
Barcode		Handcuff	
Badge		Church	
Wife		Wolf	
Chief		Roof	
Half		Scarf	

 **Activity 13: Select the most appropriate word from the list and fill in the blank by writing its correct plural form.**

Activity	Church	Flag	Quiz
Analysis	City	Framework	Scoff
Artifact	Country	Knife	Tax
Axis	Desk	Loaf	Watch
Brush	Drum	Mystery	Witness
Calf	Elf	Process	Wolf

1. The musicians set up their ______________________________ on stage, ready to kick off the evening concert.

2. The bakers placed the freshly baked ______________________________ on the counter.

3. The artist painted vivid scenes of bustling ______________________________.

4. The data were plotted along the X and Y ______________________________.

5. The farmer tended to his cattle, including the newborn ______________________________.

6. The author's new book explores ancient myths and modern ______________________________.

7. The museum showcased ancient ______________________________ from various civilizations.

Activity	Church	Flag	Quiz
Analysis	City	Framework	Scoff
Artifact	Country	Knife	Tax
Axis	Desk	Loaf	Watch
Brush	Drum	Mystery	Witness
Calf	Elf	Process	Wolf

8. The software consists of multiple ____________________________ that interact seamlessly.

9. ____________________________ from neighboring nations joined to discuss trade agreements.

10. The office was filled with neatly organized ____________________________, each equipped with a computer and a stack of files.

11. The thieves were caught after stealing priceless ____________________________.

12. They organized several fun ____________________________ for the children at the party.

13. During the parade, colorful ____________________________ representing different states were carried by the participants.

14. The ____________________________ in the story helped the shoemaker make elegant shoes.

15. The teacher ignored the ____________________________ from the students as she announced the surprise quiz.

Activity	Church	Flag	Quiz
Analysis	City	Framework	Scoff
Artifact	Country	Knife	Tax
Axis	Desk	Loaf	Watch
Brush	Drum	Mystery	Witness
Calf	Elf	Process	Wolf

16. The new software will streamline our ______________________________.

17. Researchers presented their ______________________________ at the conference.

18. The jury listened to all the ______________________________.

19. Painters cleaned their ______________________________ after finishing the mural.

20. The community organized events at local ______________________________.

21. The teacher prepared challenging ______________________________ for the students.

22. They collected antique pocket ______________________________.

23. The new law introduces higher ______________________________.

24. The ______________________________ howled in the distance under the full moon.

Activity 14: Read the sentences below. Identify whether the plural forms are correct or incorrect. If incorrect, rewrite the plural word correctly.

1. The **cat's** are playing with their toys.

☐ CORRECT   ☐ INCORRECT _________________________

2. The **student's** attended the assembly in the auditorium.

☐ CORRECT   ☐ INCORRECT _________________________

3. The **teachers** discussed their plans for the upcoming semester.

☐ CORRECT   ☐ INCORRECT _________________________

4. The **car's** in the parking lot need washing.

☐ CORRECT   ☐ INCORRECT _________________________

5. The **chair's** in the conference room are brand new.

☐ CORRECT   ☐ INCORRECT _________________________

6. The **dogs** were barking loudly in the park.

☐ CORRECT   ☐ INCORRECT _________________________

7. The **flowers** in the garden bloom every spring.

☐ CORRECT   ☐ INCORRECT _________________________

SPELLING FOR ADULTS ©2025

8. The **company's** were presenting their new ideas at the expo.

☐ CORRECT ☐ INCORRECT ____________________

9. The **players** celebrated their victory after the match.

☐ CORRECT ☐ INCORRECT ____________________

10. The **cake's** at the bakery looked delicious.

☐ CORRECT ☐ INCORRECT ____________________

11. The **phone's** on the desk need to be charged.

☐ CORRECT ☐ INCORRECT ____________________

12. The **tree's** in the orchard are full of ripe fruit.

☐ CORRECT ☐ INCORRECT ____________________

13. The **hotel's** in the city were fully booked for the event.

☐ CORRECT ☐ INCORRECT ____________________

14. The **offices** were closed for the holiday weekend.

☐ CORRECT ☐ INCORRECT ____________________

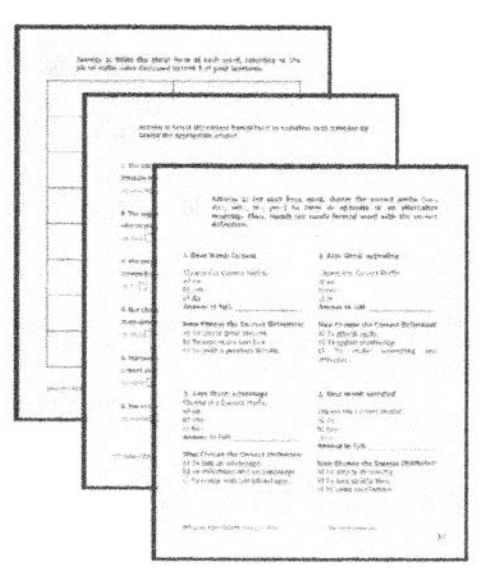

<u>Supplementary Practice Program for Adults</u>

To reinforce what you've learned in this unit, download and print the corresponding worksheets by visiting the following webpage or scanning the QR code.

https://natashascripts.com/spelling-extra-practice-adults/

Unit 3: Spelling in Syllables

Introduction
Spelling in syllables has been proven to significantly improve spelling accuracy and retention. Syllables are like beats in music, with each beat combining a vowel sound and one or more consonants. By focusing on the unique sound of each syllable, you can better understand the distinct components of a word. This process, called syllabification, helps you hear and identify individual sounds in spoken words, sharpening your listening, speaking, and reading skills by making you more attuned to sound patterns. Breaking long words into smaller syllable units also makes their spelling easier to learn and remember.

Unit Overview
The aim of this unit is to develop your ability to spell longer and more challenging words by breaking them into manageable syllables. By understanding how words are constructed through syllabification, you will enhance your spelling confidence and accuracy.

In this unit, we will practice syllabification with some of the most commonly misspelled words frequently encountered in daily life and work. Breaking these high-frequency words into syllables will help you identify tricky letter positions, double letters, and silent letters—common causes of spelling errors.

By the end of this unit, you will be able to:
1. **Break challenging words into syllables to improve spelling accuracy.**
2. **Identify tricky letters, double letters, and silent letters in commonly misspelled words.**
3. **Use syllabification to understand the structure of longer words.**
4. **Apply these words accurately in meaningful contexts.**

Supplementary Practice Program
To further reinforce the lessons in this unit, you can download the corresponding supplementary worksheets designed for extra practice. The link and QR code to access these worksheets are provided at the end of this unit.

What is a Syllable?

A syllable is a single, unbroken unit of sound in a word. This means the sound **cannot be divided further**. For example, the word *cat* is a one-syllable word—it produces a single, uninterrupted sound. Compare this to the word *caterer*, which can be broken into three distinct syllables: *ca - ter - er*. Each syllable represents a unit of sound that cannot be divided further.

As you can see, words can have one or more syllables. Every syllable contains at least one vowel sound. For example, the word *heat* has one syllable made up of a vowel sound (*ea*) combined with consonants (*h* and *t*). The word *eye* also has one syllable, but it consists entirely of a vowel sound, without any consonants.

The word *acorn*, on the other hand, has two syllables: *a - corn*. As can be seen, the vowel *a* can form a syllable on its own, producing a single unbroken sound. Another example is the word *idea* which has three unbroken sounds with *i* and *a* forming respectively a syllable on their own: *i - de - a*. While consonants are necessary for forming many words, they rely on vowels to create uninterrupted sounds. This is why **every syllable contains at least one vowel sound**.

How to Split Words into Syllables

Splitting words into syllables helps us understand their structure and pronunciation. To identify syllables, focus on the unbroken sounds—or "beats"—in a word.

Here are some tips to help you split words into syllables effectively:

1. Feel the Beats

Listen to the distinct beats in the word as you say it aloud. Each beat corresponds to a syllable. You can tap your hand or clap to mark the beats. For example:

- The word *umbrella* has three beats: *um – brel – la.*
- The word *accident* has three beats: *ac – ci – dent.*
- The word *demonstrative* has four beats: *de – mon – stra – tive.*

2. Spot Consonant-Vowel Patterns

Understanding consonant-vowel patterns can help you identify where syllables begin and end. Words are often made up of repeating units of vowels and consonants, and these patterns provide clues for splitting the word into syllables:

- **Vowel-Consonant (VC)**: A vowel followed by a consonant often marks the end of a syllable.
    - Example: open → o – pen.

- **Consonant-Vowel (CV)**: A consonant followed by a vowel typically starts a new syllable.
    - Example: robot → ro – bot.

- **Consonant-Vowel-Consonant (CVC)**: A vowel surrounded by consonants usually forms one syllable.
    - Example: basket → bas – ket.

- **Double Consonants (CC)**: When two identical consonants appear together, they are split between syllables.
    - Example: rabbit → rab – bit.

- **Vowel-Alone**: A vowel can sometimes form its own syllable when it produces a separate sound.
    - Example: area → ar – e – a.

3. Listen for Vowel Sounds

Every syllable contains at least one vowel sound (*a, e, i, o, u*, and sometimes *y*). Identify the vowels in a word and their surrounding consonants. This will help you understand how the syllables naturally divide.

Why Syllabification Matters for Spelling

Syllabification helps you break longer and more complex words into smaller, manageable parts. More importantly, it sharpens your focus on these smaller parts, allowing you to connect the sounds each syllable produces with how it is written. By practicing syllabification, you actively engage both your eyes and ears, tuning into the sounds and visual patterns of words simultaneously.

English spelling combines the challenge of hearing the sounds produced by letters in each syllable and understanding how those sounds are represented in writing. Syllabification lets you feel the rhythm and sound of each syllable while visually focusing on its written form.

By acquiring and practicing this skill, you train your brain to engage more deeply with words. Over time, you'll find yourself spelling more accurately because you've developed the ability to break words into their smaller parts and focus on them with precision.

In the following activities, you will first practice syllabifying and spelling commonly misspelled high-frequency words. You will then apply these words in a fill-in-the-blank exercise and a multiple-choice spelling activity.

Each word will be displayed in a slightly larger font to enhance visibility and focus, allowing you to underline or circle any tricky letters. Next, you'll practice writing the word in syllable form and as a whole.

Because spelling words in context greatly enhances retention, the activity following syllabification will focus on practicing spelling the words correctly and placing them in the appropriate context. This dual focus on spelling and usage will ensure you internalize both the spelling and meaning of each word.

 **Activity 15: Write each word in its syllabified form and then as a whole word. Use the lightbulb row to highlight any tricky letters.**

1. Absence

ab – sence

_______________   _______________

absence

_______________   _______________

3. Acquire

ac – quire

_______________   _______________

acquire

_______________   _______________

2. Accommodate

ac – com – mod – ate

____

____

accommodate

____

____

4. Awkward

awk – ward

_______________   _______________

awkward

_______________   _______________

5 . B e g i n n i n g

be – gin – ning

____

____

beginning

____

____

7 . C a l e n d a r

cal – en – dar

____

____

calendar

____

____

6 . B e l i e v e

be – lieve

____

____

believe

____

____

8 . C o l l e a g u e

col – league

____

____

colleague

____

____

9. Conscience

con – science

____

____

conscience

____

____

10. Conscious

con – scious

____

____

conscious

____

____

11. Definitely

def – i – nite – ly

____

____

definitely

____

____

12. Desperate

des – per – ate

____

____

desperate

____

____

13. Embarrass

em - bar - rass

____

____

embarrass

____

____

14. Exaggerate

ex - ag - ger - ate

____

____

exaggerate

____

____

15. Foresee

fore - see

____

____

foresee

____

____

16. Judgment

judg - ment

____

____

judgment

____

____

17. Necessary

nec – es – sa – ry

____

____

necessary

____

____

18. Recommend

rec – om – mend

____

____

recommend

____

____

19. Separate

sep – a – rate

____

____

separate

____

____

20. Successful

suc – cess – ful

____

____

successful

____

____

 **Activity 16: Fill in the blanks with the most appropriate word from the word bank provided. Use the context of the passage to guide your choices.**

Acknowledge	Conscience	Judgment
Acquire	Conscious	Necessary
Awkward	Definitely	Recommend
Calendar	Exaggerate	Successful
Colleagues	Foresee	

How to Be a Successful Professional in Today's Workplace

Starting a new job can feel _____________________ at the beginning, but with the right mindset and strategies, you can _____________________ the skills and confidence needed to excel. It's _____________________ to _____________________ your own strengths and areas for improvement, as well as to _____________________ in your potential for growth.

One critical skill is time management, so keeping a well-organized _____________________ is a must. Being punctual and prepared shows your _____________________ that you value their time. Additionally, clear _____________________ and the ability to _____________________ potential challenges are key to making _____________________ decisions in the workplace.

Acknowledge   **Conscience**   **Judgment**

Acquire   **Conscious**   **Necessary**

Awkward   **Definitely**   **Recommend**

Calendar   **Exaggerate**   **Successful**

Colleagues   **Foresee**

Maintaining professionalism also requires staying _________________________ of your actions and their impact on others. A strong _____________________ will guide you in treating others with respect and integrity. Avoid the temptation to _______________________ achievements; honesty will earn you lasting trust.

If you're unsure about a decision, it's always wise to seek advice. Experts often _______________________ consulting trusted mentors or colleagues. Don't be afraid to ask for help—it's not a sign of weakness but a step toward improvement.

Mistakes are part of the journey, and learning to take responsibility for them shows maturity and resilience. Owning up to a missed deadline or clarifying a misunderstanding directly will earn you respect and demonstrate maturity.

By following these principles, you'll _______________________ set yourself on the path to success, both personally and professionally.

 # Activity 17: Read each definition carefully and choose the correctly spelled word from the options provided.

1. To divide or cause to divide into different parts or sections.

A. seperete

B. seperate

C. separete

D. separate

2. To feel self-conscious or ashamed.

A. embarras

B. embarrass

C. embarass

D. emberass

3. The state of being away or not present.

A. absense

B. abscence

C. absence

D. absance

4. Feeling or showing great urgency or need.

A. desperet

B. disperate

C. desparate

D. desperate

5. To accept something as true, genuine, or real.

A. believe

B. beleive

C. belive

D. beleave

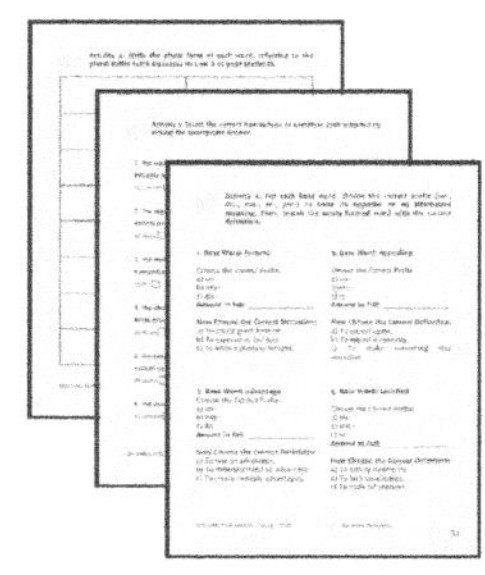

PROGRESS PORTAL 1: Reflect and Assess

Well done on completing Module One!

You've worked through 14 lessons across three units, tackling tricky homophones, plurals, and syllables. Take a moment to celebrate your hard work —it's a big achievement!

Now, it's time to check your progress in the Progress Portal. Follow the steps below to:

- Take the online test to assess what you've mastered.
- Identify areas where extra practice might help.
- Set new study goals for the next module.

Step 1: Take the assessment online by scanning the QR code or visiting https://natashascripts.com/progressportals/

Password for Progress Portal 1, Assessment 1: **BuildingSkills1-3**

Step 2: Review your results and record your score and test date on the next page.

Step 3: Reflect on your progress and plan your next steps by completing the prompts below.

Assessment 1

Score:

____

Date:

____

Reflection

1. What concepts or skills from Units 1–3 do you feel confident about?

2. Which areas or topics do you find most challenging, and why?

3. What strategy can you use to improve in these areas?
(*E.g., review examples or practice tricky words daily.*)

Goal-Setting

1. Write down one specific goal you want to achieve before completing the next three units. (*E.g.,* "*Master the spelling of homophones by practicing 10 sentences daily.*")

2. What steps will you take to achieve this goal? (*E.g., Use the supplementary practice file, revisit unit examples, or create personal memory aids.*)

3. How will you measure your success? (*E.g., Taking the online test multiple times until I achieve a score above 70%.*)

MODULE 2:

Spelling Patterns with Prefixes, Suffixes and Phonograms

Unit 4: Decoding Words with the Prefixes *un-*, *dis-*, *mis-*, *re-*, and *pre-*

Introduction
This unit focuses on a set of essential and widely used prefixes that play a pivotal role in academic, professional, and everyday communication. Understanding and mastering the prefixes *un-*, *dis-*, *mis-*, *re-*, and *pre-* will enhance your ability to decode unfamiliar vocabulary and enrich your command of the language. The words featured in this unit are intermediate to advanced in difficulty, offering a stimulating challenge that will build your spelling proficiency and expand your vocabulary.

Unit Overview
In this unit, you will explore the function and meaning of each prefix through clear explanations and examples across different parts of speech, including adjectives, verbs, and nouns. After gaining an understanding of each prefix's role, you will engage in targeted spelling drills and fill-in-the-blank exercises to practice applying these prefixes to selected high-frequency words. These words have been carefully chosen for their relevance to work, academic, and everyday contexts.

Recognizing that the exercises in this unit may sometimes feel extensive, a break page has been included between practice activities. This page provides a link and QR code for downloading free crossword and word search puzzles that will refresh your focus.

By the end of this unit, you will be able to:
- **Understand the function of the prefixes *un-*, *dis-*, *mis-*, *re-*, and *pre-*.**
- **Accurately spell and apply a selection of high-frequency prefixed words.**

Supplementary Practice Program
As you work through the lessons in this unit, you might want to jot down challenging words. The supplementary worksheets for this unit include a dedicated spelling page for recording these words. You can access the worksheets via the link and QR code provided at the end of this unit.

Lesson 15: The Prefixes *un-* and *dis-*

	PREFIX	
A prefix is added to the <u>beginning</u> of a word to <u>change its meaning</u>.		

PREFIX	FUNCTION	EXAMPLES
Un-	• Creates the opposite meaning of the base word, typically an adjective or a verb. • Indicates negation or the reversal of an action.	<u>*Adjectives*</u> <u>*Verbs*</u> *unnecessary* *unravel* *unsuccessful* *unsubscribe* *unbelievable* *unfasten* *unusual* *unload*
Dis-	• Creates the opposite meaning of the base word, which can be an adjective, verb or noun. • Forms words that indicate negation, opposition, or reversal of an action or state. • Often implies removal or separation, as in disconnect or disassemble.	<u>*Adjectives*</u> <u>*Verbs*</u> *disagreeable* *disagree* *disorganized* *discontinue* *dishonest* *disappear* *disheartened* *disrespect* <u>*Nouns*</u> *disagreement* *disadvantage* *disconnection* *disapproval*

Note: While "dis-" often indicates negation, opposition, or reversal, not all words starting with "dis-" follow this pattern. For example, "disperse" and "distract" do not convey negation or opposition. Additionally, some words with "dis-" have base words that no longer exist independently in modern English, such as "rupt" in "disrupt." In other cases, like "tract" in "distract," the base word does exist independently, but its meaning is unrelated to the meaning of "distract."

  SPELLING FOR ADULTS ©2025

 **Activity 18: Study and spell each of the following *un*-prefixed words, commonly used in daily life and work, and often misspelled. You will practice using these words in the next activity.**

Unaddressed ______________________ ______________________

Unappealing ______________________ ______________________

Unapproachable ______________________ ______________________

Unattainable ______________________ ______________________

Unavailable ______________________ ______________________

Unbelievable ______________________ ______________________

Uncontrollable ______________________ ______________________

Unforgettable ______________________ ______________________

Unimaginable ______________________ ______________________

Unintelligible ______________________ ______________________

Unmanageable ____________________ ____________________

Unnecessary ____________________ ____________________

Unnoticeable ____________________ ____________________

Unparalleled ____________________ ____________________

Unpredictable ____________________ ____________________

Unquestionable ____________________ ____________________

Unreliable ____________________ ____________________

Unsettling ____________________ ____________________

Unsuccessful ____________________ ____________________

Unusual ____________________ ____________________

 **Activity 19: Fill in the blanks with the most appropriate word from the word bank provided. Use the context of the sentence to guide your choices.**

Unaddressed	Unbelievable	Unmanageable	Unquestionable
Unappealing	Uncontrollable	Unnecessary	Unreliable
Unapproachable	Unforgettable	Unnoticeable	Unsettling
Unattainable	Unimaginable	Unparalleled	Unsuccessful
Unavailable	Unintelligible	Unpredictable	Unusual

1. The speaker's rapid delivery and heavy accent rendered his presentation almost ______________________________ to the audience.

2. Depending on ______________________________ public transportation often made her late for work.

3. The renowned artist was so private and ______________________________ that even his closest colleagues rarely saw his work in progress.

4. It was ______________________________to see snow in April, even for a region known for its unpredictable weather.

5. Visiting the ancient ruins of Machu Picchu was an ______________________________experience that left the travelers in awe.

6. Many environmental issues remain ______________________________, despite growing evidence of their impact on global health.

7. The ______________________________ weather in the mountains made planning the hike a challenge.

Unaddressed   Unbelievable   Unmanageable   Unquestionable

Unappealing   Uncontrollable   Unnecessary   Unreliable

Unapproachable   Unforgettable   Unnoticeable   Unsettling

Unattainable   Unimaginable   Unparalleled   Unsuccessful

Unavailable   Unintelligible   Unpredictable   Unusual

8. For centuries, the idea of human flight seemed ___________________________, until the Wright brothers achieved it in 1903.

9. The restoration of the historic painting was so seamless that the repairs were ___________________________ even to art experts.

10. The ___________________________ resilience of people during natural disasters often becomes a source of global inspiration.

11. The outdated design of the office space was so ___________________________ that employees avoided using the break room entirely.

12. Despite multiple attempts, their efforts to reach a compromise remained ___________________________.

13. The sudden and ___________________________laughter of the audience turned the serious lecture into a comedic event.

14. The company's rapid growth led to an ___________________________workload for its under-resourced teams.

15. The heated argument over seating arrangements felt entirely ___________________________ during such an important meeting.

Unaddressed	Unbelievable	Unmanageable	Unquestionable
Unappealing	Uncontrollable	Unnecessary	Unreliable
Unapproachable	Unforgettable	Unnoticeable	Unsettling
Unattainable	Unimaginable	Unparalleled	Unsuccessful
Unavailable	Unintelligible	Unpredictable	Unusual

16. The eerie silence in the abandoned house was deeply ________________________ to the group of explorers.

17. Her leadership during the crisis was ________________________, setting a standard for others to follow.

18. His ________________________ dedication to the project earned him the admiration of his peers.

19. Advances in artificial intelligence have opened doors to ________________________ possibilities in medicine and technology.

20. The manager apologized profusely when the requested files were ________________________ due to a system crash.

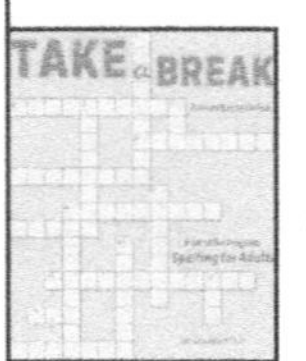

Need a break? Head over to the Take a Break page for free fun crossword and word search puzzles created just for you. Scan the QR code or visit the link below to get started!

https://natashascripts.com/takeabreak-spelling-puzzles/

 **Activity 20: Study and spell each of the following _dis-_ prefixed words, commonly used in daily life and work, and often misspelled. You will practice using these words in the next activity.**

Disadvantage _______________________   _______________________

Disagreeable _______________________   _______________________

Disapprove _______________________   _______________________

Disassemble _______________________   _______________________

Disbelief _______________________   _______________________

Discontinue _______________________   _______________________

Disengage _______________________   _______________________

Disheartened _______________________   _______________________

Dishonest _______________________   _______________________

   SPELLING FOR ADULTS ©2025

Disorganized   ________________________   ________________________

Disregard   ________________________   ________________________

Dissatisfied   ________________________   ________________________

Activity 21: Fill in the blanks with the most appropriate word from the word bank provided. Use the context of the sentence to guide your choices.

Disadvantage(s)	Discontinue	Disregard
Disagreeable	Disengage	Dissatisfied
Disapprove	Disheartened	
Disassemble	Dishonest	
Disbelief	Disorganized	

1. Her manager seemed to ____________________________ of the casual tone she used in the formal email.

2. The team felt ________________________ after their hard work on the project went unnoticed during the presentation.

3. Many customers were ________________________ with the product's quality, leaving critical reviews online.

Disadvantage(s)	Discontinue	Disregard
Disagreeable	Disengage	Dissatisfied
Disapprove	Disheartened	
Disassemble	Dishonest	
Disbelief	Disorganized	

4. In the 19th century, women faced significant _________________________

in accessing education and professional opportunities.

5. The gallery's _________________________ layout made it difficult for

visitors to fully appreciate the artwork on display.

6. Due to declining sales, the company decided to

_________________________ its line of luxury notebooks.

7. The scientist's groundbreaking discovery was met with

_________________________ until further experiments confirmed the

results.

8. His _________________________ for safety protocols led to an accident on

the construction site.

9. The artist's unconventional style was initially deemed

_________________________ by critics, only to be celebrated decades later.

10. The politician's _________________________ claims were quickly

debunked by investigative journalists.

11. In high-stress situations, it's important to _________________________

from heated arguments to maintain professionalism.

12. The mechanic had to _________________________ the engine to

identify the source of the unusual noise.

Lesson 16: The Prefixes *mis-*, *re-*, and *pre-*

PREFIX	FUNCTION	EXAMPLES

Mis-	• Often implies something is done incorrectly, badly or wrongly, when added to a verb or noun.
	• Commonly used to indicate:
	  ◦ Errors or mistakes
	  ◦ Wrong or inappropriate action
	  ◦ Misuse or improper application
	  ◦ Failure or deficiency
		Verbs *Nouns*
		misinterpret *miscalculation*
		misdirect *misconduct*
		misspell *misinformation*
		mismanage *mismanagement*

Re-	• Typically used with verbs to indicate doing something again or repeating an action. • May also indicate a return to a previous state, position or direction, implying "back" or "backward."	*Verbs* *renew* *rebuild* *regenerate* *review* *recall* *retract*
Pre-	• Indicates something occurring before in time, place, or order, often related to planning, earlier sequences, or anticipation. • Words starting with this prefix are usually adjectives, verbs, or nouns.	*Adjectives* *Verbs* *predetermined* *predetermine* *prehistoric* *prearrange* *premature* *preheat* *precautionary* *prepay* *Nouns* *predetermination* *preview* *prerequisite*

Note: While "pre-" often attaches to standalone base words to indicate "before" in time, place, or order, some base words, like "monition" in "premonition" and "pare" in "prepare," no longer exist independently in modern English. Yet, "pre-" still conveys its meaning of "before" in such cases.

Non-Standalone Words
preliminary (adj.)
preclude (v.)
prejudice (n.)

How do we determine whether to use *un-*, *dis-*, or *mis-*, since all three prefixes convey negation or opposition?

1. Understand the Context and Convention:
- If the base word already exists with one of these prefixes, use the conventionally accepted form (e.g., *unhappy*, not *dishappy* or *mishappy*).

2. Consider the Nuance:
- Use *un-* for neutral opposites (e.g., *unplug, undo, untie*).
- Use *dis-* for active undoing or strong opposition (e.g., *disconnect, disagree, disregard*).
- Use *mis-* for actions done incorrectly or in error (e.g., *misjudge, misapply, misinterpret*).

3. Practice Common Words:
- Some prefixes are simply part of a word's accepted spelling, and these words should be practiced and memorized.

 **Activity 22: Study and spell each of the following *mis*-prefixed words, commonly used in daily life and work, and often misspelled. You will practice using these words in the next activity.**

Misaligned

Miscalculation

Misconduct

Misfortune

Misguided

Misinformation

Misinterpret

Misjudge

Mislead

Mismanage

Misrepresent _______________________ _______________________

Misspell _______________________ _______________________

Misunderstood _______________________ _______________________

Misuse _______________________ _______________________

 **Activity 23: Fill in the blanks with the most appropriate word from the word bank provided. Use the context of the sentence to guide your choices.**

Misaligned	**Misinformation**	**Misrepresent**
Miscalculation	**Misinterpret**	**Misspell**
Misconduct	**Misjudge**	**Misunderstood**
Misfortune	**Mislead**	**Misuse**
Misguided	**Mismanage**	

1. Her _______________________ attempt to solve the problem only made the situation more complicated for everyone involved.

2. Vincent van Gogh's art was largely _______________________ during his lifetime but is celebrated today for its genius.

3. The architect realized the beams were _______________________, causing structural concerns in the historic building.

     SPELLING FOR ADULTS ©2025

Misaligned   **Misinformation**   **Misrepresent**

Miscalculation   **Misinterpret**   **Misspell**

Misconduct   **Misjudge**   **Misunderstood**

Misfortune   **Mislead**   **Misuse**

Misguided   **Mismanage**

4. It's easy to ______________________________ someone's intentions when you're relying solely on text messages without context.

5. The employee was dismissed for repeated ________________________________, which disrupted the office environment.

6. If you ______________________________ key terms in your resume, it could give employers the wrong impression about your attention to detail.

7. The spread of ______________________________on social media contributed to confusion about the event's start time.

8. The CEO ______________________________the corporation's funds, diverting them to risky investments and leaving the company in a precarious financial situation.

9. A ______________________________in the budget left the museum project short on funds, delaying the exhibit's opening.

10. The scientist was criticized for attempting to ______________________________ the data to support a flawed hypothesis.

11. The ______________________________of a sudden engine failure forced the pilot to make an emergency landing.

Misaligned	Misinformation	Misrepresent
Miscalculation	Misinterpret	Misspell
Misconduct	Misjudge	Misunderstood
Misfortune	Mislead	Misuse
Misguided	Mismanage	

12. The email was so brief that it was easy to _________________________________
the tone as rude instead of urgent.

13. The flashy advertisement was designed to _________________________________
consumers into thinking the product was a miracle cure.

14. The lawyer warned her client not to _________________________________the
facts during the negotiation, as it could backfire in court.

Activity 24: Study and spell each of the following *re-*prefixed words, commonly used in daily life and work, and often misspelled. You will practice using these words in the next activity.

Rebuild ________________________   ________________________

Recharge ________________________   ________________________

Reconnect ________________________   ________________________

Reconsider ________________________   ________________________

Recover

Reevaluate

Refill

Relive

Relocate

Remind

Renew

Reorganize

Repair

Repeat

Replace

Restart

Return ______________________ ______________________

Revise ______________________ ______________________

Revisit ______________________ ______________________

Rewrite ______________________ ______________________

Need a break? Head over to the Take a Break page for free fun crossword and word search puzzles created just for you. Scan the QR code or visit the link below to get started!

https://natashascripts.com/takeabreak-spelling-puzzles/

SPELLING FOR ADULTS ©2025

 **Activity 25: Study and spell each of the following _pre-_ prefixed words, commonly used in daily life and work, and often misspelled. You will practice using these words in the next activity.**

Preapprove ___________________________   ___________________________

Prearrange ___________________________   ___________________________

Precaution ___________________________   ___________________________

Preclude ___________________________   ___________________________

Precook ___________________________   ___________________________

Predefine ___________________________   ___________________________

Predict ___________________________   ___________________________

Preheat ___________________________   ___________________________

Preload ____________________ ____________________

Prepare ____________________ ____________________

Prepay ____________________ ____________________

Presuppose ____________________ ____________________

Prerequisite ____________________ ____________________

Preschedule ____________________ ____________________

Preserve ____________________ ____________________

Presume ____________________ ____________________

Pretest ____________________ ____________________

Prevent ____________________ ____________________

Preview ____________________ ____________________

Activity 26: Fill in the blanks with the most appropriate word from the word bank provided. Use the context of the sentence to guide your choices.

preapprove	prerequisite	reevaluate	renew
prearrange	presume	refill	reorganize
precaution	pretest	relive	revise
preclude	preview	relocate	rewrite
preload	reconnect		

1. The documentary allowed viewers to _______________________________ the pivotal moments of the civil rights movement.

2. A solid understanding of art history is a _______________________________ for enrolling in the advanced curatorial course.

3. The library decided to _______________________________ its collection by genre to improve accessibility for readers.

4. The bank agreed to _______________________________ his mortgage application, saving him time when house hunting.

5. The playwright had to _______________________________ the ending after early feedback from the test audience.

6. As a _______________________________, the museum installed climate control systems to preserve the ancient artifacts.

7. The annual reunion was the perfect opportunity to _______________________________ with former colleagues.

preapprove	prerequisite	reevaluate	renew
prearrange	presume	refill	reorganize
precaution	pretest	relive	revise
preclude	preview	relocate	rewrite
preload	reconnect		

8. The editor invited the team to _____________________________ the final layout of the magazine before publication.

9. After ten years in the city, they decided to _____________________________ to a quieter rural area.

10. His prior commitments will _____________________________ him from attending the conference next week.

11. They decided to _____________________________ the seating for the gallery opening to ensure a smooth event.

12. After the unexpected delays, the project team decided to _____________________________ their timeline and priorities.

13. He took extra time to _____________________________ his proposal before submitting it to the grant committee.

14. The IT department will _____________________________ the software onto all new employee laptops.

15. She stopped at the café to _____________________________her thermos before heading to the office.

16. The engineering firm conducted a _____________________________ of the materials to ensure safety standards were met.

17. The artist used her travels to _____________________________ her creative inspiration for the upcoming exhibit.

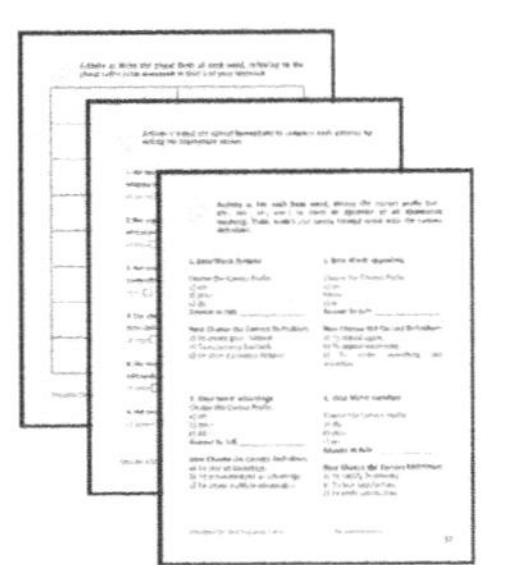

<u>Supplementary Practice Program for Adults</u>

To reinforce what you've learned in this unit, download and print the corresponding worksheets by visiting the following webpage or scanning the QR code.

https://natashascripts.com/spelling-extra-practice-adults/

Unit 5: Rules and Patterns for *-ed* and *-ing* Suffixes

Introduction
The lessons in this unit focus on two fundamental suffixes that you encounter constantly in English—the -ed and -ing endings. Although these suffixes appear straightforward, the challenge often lies in how the base word transforms when one of these endings is added, such as doubling the final consonant or dropping the final e.

Unit Overview
The spelling rules and conventions presented in this unit are supported by tables that simplify the process of understanding and applying these patterns. Take your time with each word in the tables, carefully noting any difficult letter changes. Paying close attention to these details will reinforce your grasp of the underlying spelling patterns.

In this unit, you will be able to:
- **Explore how the *-ed* and *-ing* suffixes modify base words.**
- **Identify the properties of base words to determine the appropriate spelling rule for adding these endings.**
- **Spell academic and professional vocabulary that incorporates these suffixes.**
- **Apply these suffixes in context to enhance your vocabulary and writing skills.**

Supplementary Practice Program
To further reinforce the lessons in this unit, you can download the corresponding supplementary worksheets designed for extra practice. The link and QR code to access these worksheets are provided at the end of this unit.

SUFFIX

A suffix is added to the <u>end</u> of a word to <u>change its form or meaning</u>.

Examples: brush**es**, danc**ed**, runn**ing**, writ**er**, discov**ery**, secret**ary**, direct**or**, repet**ition**, confu**sion**, home**less**, care**ful**,

When do we double the final consonant when adding *-ed* or *-ing*?

<u>Rule 1</u>

Double the final consonant when adding *-ed* or *-ing* if:

- The word has only **one syllable**, and
- It ends with the pattern **consonant + vowel + consonant** (CVC).

One Syllable + CVC	+ed	+ing
Beg	Begged	Begging
Bin	Binned	Binning
Tap	Tapped	Tapping
Map	Mapped	Mapping
Plan	Planned	Planning
Step	Stepped	Stepping
Slip	Slipped	Slipping
Hop	Hopped	Hopping
Stop	Stopped	Stopping

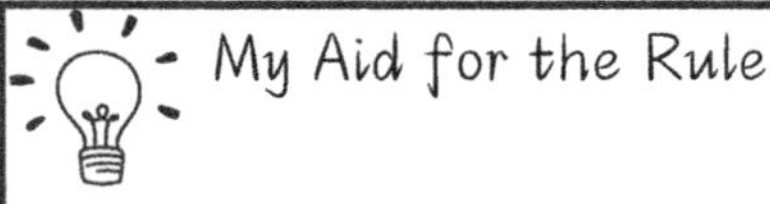

My Aid for the Rule

<u>Rule 2</u>
Double the final consonant when adding *-ed* or *-ing* if:
- The word has **more than one syllable**,
- It ends with the pattern **consonant + vowel + consonant**, and
- The final syllable before the suffix is **accented**.

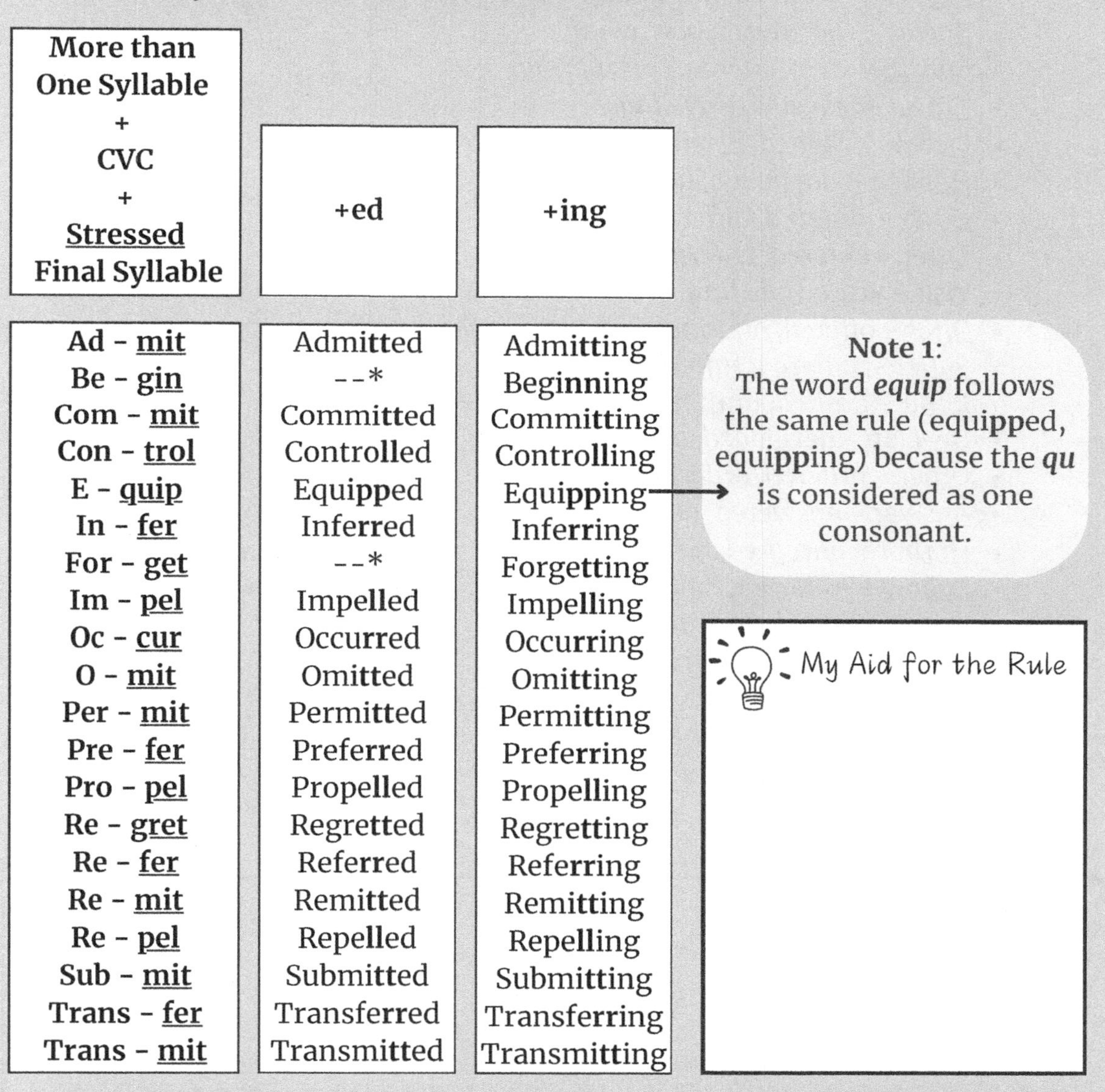

More than One Syllable + CVC + <u>Stressed</u> Final Syllable	+ed	+ing
Ad – <u>mit</u>	Admitted	Admitting
Be – <u>gin</u>	– – *	Beginning
Com – <u>mit</u>	Committed	Committing
Con – <u>trol</u>	Controlled	Controlling
E – <u>quip</u>	Equipped	Equipping
In – <u>fer</u>	Inferred	Inferring
For – <u>get</u>	– – *	Forgetting
Im – <u>pel</u>	Impelled	Impelling
Oc – <u>cur</u>	Occurred	Occurring
O – <u>mit</u>	Omitted	Omitting
Per – <u>mit</u>	Permitted	Permitting
Pre – <u>fer</u>	Preferred	Preferring
Pro – <u>pel</u>	Propelled	Propelling
Re – <u>gret</u>	Regretted	Regretting
Re – <u>fer</u>	Referred	Referring
Re – <u>mit</u>	Remitted	Remitting
Re – <u>pel</u>	Repelled	Repelling
Sub – <u>mit</u>	Submitted	Submitting
Trans – <u>fer</u>	Transferred	Transferring
Trans – <u>mit</u>	Transmitted	Transmitting

*Irregular verb that does not take *-ed.*

SPELLING FOR ADULTS ©2025

Note 2:
When the <u>accent</u> does **not** fall on the final syllable, the final consonant is **not doubled**.

Examples:
- <u>Hin</u>der – hindered, hindering.
- <u>Bor</u>row – borrowed, borrowing.
- Con<u>sid</u>er – considered, considering.
- <u>Tra</u>vel – traveled, traveling.
- <u>Lis</u>ten – listened, listening.
- <u>Hap</u>pen – happened, happening.
- <u>Dif</u>fer – differed, differing.
- <u>En</u>ter – entered, entering.
- <u>Vis</u>it – visited, visiting.
- <u>Of</u>fer – offered, offering.
- <u>Suf</u>fer – suffered, suffering.
- <u>Lim</u>it – limited, limiting.
- <u>De</u>velop – developed, developing.
- <u>Or</u>der – ordered, ordering.
- <u>An</u>swer – answered, answered.
- <u>Har</u>bor – harbored, harboring.
- <u>Fol</u>low – followed, following.
- <u>O</u>pen – opened, opening.
- <u>Cov</u>er – covered, covering.
- <u>E</u>dit – edited, editing.
- <u>Shel</u>ter – sheltered, sheltering.

My Aid for the Rule

<u>Rule 3</u>
Rules 1 and 2 apply to most words when adding a suffix beginning with a **vowel** (vowel suffix).

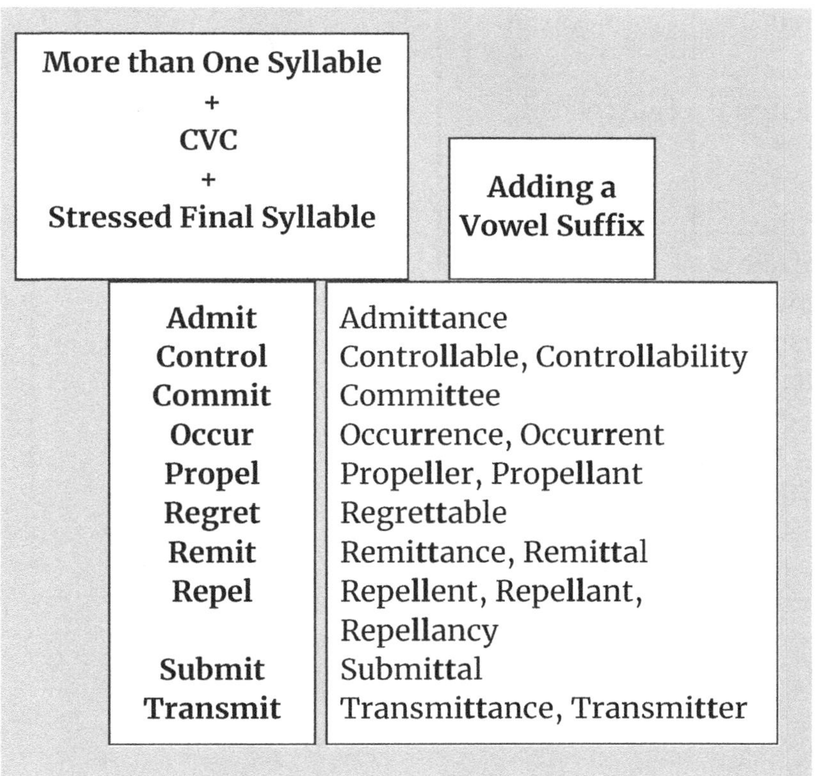

Note 1:
When the suffix added is a consonant suffix, this rule does not apply:
E.g.,
- *commitment*
- *regretful*
- *regretfully*

The following words are exceptions to this rule and their spelling should be studied:

- *Refer – reference.*

- *Prefer – preferable, preference.*

- *Transfer – transferable, transferability, transferal.*

SPELLING FOR ADULTS ©2025

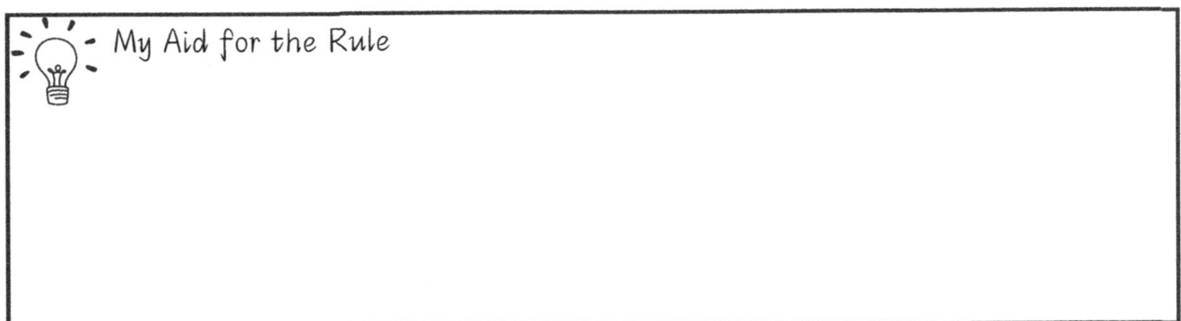

Rule 4

Do not double the final consonant when adding *-ed* or *-ing* if:

- The word ends in **more than one consonant**.

More than One Consonant	+ed	+ing
Arre<u>st</u>	Arrested	Arresting
Bui<u>ld</u>	– – *	Building
Cat<u>ch</u>	– – *	Catching
Com<u>b</u>	Combed	Combing
Dri<u>ft</u>	Drifted	Drifting
Pri<u>nt</u>	Printed	Printing
Gra<u>sp</u>	Grasped	Grasping
Scrat<u>ch</u>	Scratched	Scratching
Sta<u>nd</u>	– – *	Standing
Spe<u>nd</u>	– – *	Spending
Fulfi<u>ll</u>	Fulfilled	Fulfilling
Pre<u>ss</u>	Pressed	Pressing
Sme<u>ll</u>	Smelled	Smelling

*Irregular verb that does not take *-ed*.

Activity 27: Sort the words into the correct column based on their patterns. Take your time to carefully identify each word's properties and apply the rules from this unit. Allow approximately 30 minutes to complete the exercise.

Permit	Begin	Transfer	Forget	Regret	Catch
Prefer	Commit	Transmit	Impel	Refer	Comb
Propel	Plan	Stand	Occur	Remit	Scratch
Drift	Step	Spend	Arrest	Follow	Smell
Print	Slip	Fulfill	Build	Open	
Grasp	Answer	Press	Bin	Cover	
Travel	Harbor	Hinder	Tap	Edit	
Listen	Repel	Borrow	Differ	Control	
Happen	Submit	Consider	Enter	Equip	
Admit		Infer	Visit	Omit	

One Syllable + CVC	Ends in More than one Consonant	More than One Syllable + CVC + Stressed Final Syllable	More than One Syllable + CVC + Non-Stressed Final Syllable

SPELLING FOR ADULTS ©2025

Permit	Begin	Transfer	Forget	Regret	Catch
Prefer	Commit	Transmit	Impel	Refer	Comb
Propel	Plan	Stand	Occur	Remit	Scratch
Drift	Step	Spend	Arrest	Follow	Smell
Print	Slip	Fulfill	Build	Open	
Grasp	Answer	Press	Bin	Cover	
Travel	Harbor	Hinder	Tap	Edit	
Listen	Repel	Borrow	Differ	Control	
Happen	Submit	Consider	Enter	Equip	
Admit		Infer	Visit	Omit	

One Syllable + CVC	Ends in More than one Consonant	More than One Syllable + CVC + Stressed Final Syllable	More than One Syllable + CVC + Non-Stressed Final Syllable

 **Activity 28: Complete the email below by selecting the appropriate word from the list provided and adding the suffix *-ed* or *-ing* as needed to ensure it fits correctly in the context.**

Cover Edit Equip Follow   Remit Stand Transfer Transmit

Subject: **Follow-Up on Project Transfer and Next Steps**

Dear David,

I regret the delay in _______________________the revised project plan; we encountered some unforeseen challenges in finalizing the document. However, the updated files have now been ______________________ to your department for review. Please find them attached for your reference. I've also included an ______________________summary of the key points for your convenience.

Moving forward, we are considering ______________________ the team with additional resources to avoid any hindrance to the project's timeline. I recommend ______________________ up with the finance department regarding the ______________________ funds for the next phase. It's essential to ensure that all expenses are fully ______________________ to fulfill the remaining deliverables on schedule.

If you need clarification on any aspect, feel free to refer back to the notes provided or reach out directly. I'll be ______________________ by to assist with any questions or additional considerations. Thank you for your patience and continued support in ensuring the success of this project.

Best regards,
Claire

   SPELLING FOR ADULTS ©2025

 **Activity 29: Complete the paragraphs below by selecting the appropriate word from the provided list for each paragraph and adding the suffix -ed or -ing as needed to fit the context correctly.**

Control Omit Press Regret Spend Transmit

1. After _________________________ weeks on the project, we _________________________ not considering all the potential challenges that could hinder our progress. By _________________________ key details in the initial report, we inadvertently delayed the _________________________ of critical information to stakeholders. Moving forward, we are _________________________ for stricter timelines and _________________________ resources more effectively to fulfill the remaining objectives without further setbacks.

Develop Enter Fulfill Map Suffer

2. During the 19th century, several nations _________________________ innovative cartographic techniques, which greatly improved the accuracy of _________________________ uncharted territories. Explorers often _________________________ hardships as they _________________________ harsh climates to gather data, yet their perseverance _________________________ humanity's thirst for knowledge.

Begin Commit Listen Plan Print Propel Slip Submit Travel

3. After _______________________ his journey as an amateur photographer, Tyler quickly found himself _______________________ more time and energy to the craft. What started as a hobby soon _______________________ him into a world of creativity and discovery. On weekends, he could often be found _______________________ to scenic locations, camera in hand, _______________________ to the sounds of nature while carefully _______________________ his next shot. The unpredictability of capturing the perfect moment often _______________________ through his grasp, but he never gave up. Instead, he _______________________ his best work to local galleries, gaining valuable feedback and recognition. Each photograph he _______________________ told a story. The results were truly worth the effort, as his portfolio became a visual diary of his artistic growth.

Admit Commit Plan Propel Slip Step

4. Jessica _______________________ herself to a new routine of morning exercise to improve her health. Each day, she began with a series of stretches before _______________________ onto the treadmill. Gradually, she managed to increase her endurance, _______________________ by her determination to meet her fitness goals. The schedule was carefully _______________________, with rest days to allow her body to recover. Occasionally, she _______________________ on maintaining consistency, but her perseverance kept her on track. By the end of the month, she felt accomplished, having _______________________ that her hard work was starting to pay off.

Lesson 18: The Final *-e* Rule with *-ed* and *-ing*

> **Do we keep or drop the final *e* when adding the suffixes *-ed* or *-ing*?**

<u>Rule 5</u>

- When the base word ends with a silent *-e*, <u>drop</u> the *e* before adding *-ed* or *-ing*.

Base Word	+ed	+ing	Drop the *e* and add *-ed, -ing*
Move	Moved	Moving	Mov + ed/ing
Hope	Hoped	Hoping	Hop + ed/ing
Change	Changed	Changing	Chang + ed/ing
Believe	Believed	Believing	Believ + ed/ing
Analyze	Analyzed	Analyzing	Analyz + ed/ing
Calculate	Calculated	Calculating	Calculat + ed/ing
Collaborate	Collaborated	Collaborating	Collaborat + ed/ing
Communicate	Communicated	Communicating	Communicat + ed/ing
Conclude	Concluded	Concluding	Conclud + ed/ing
Contribute	Contributed	Contributing	Contribut + ed/ing
Debate	Debated	Debating	Debat + ed/ing
Delegate	Delegated	Delegating	Delegat + ed/ing
Demonstrate	Demonstrated	Demonstrating	Demonstrat + ed/ing
Differentiate	Differentiated	Differentiating	Differentiat + ed/ing
Educate	Educated	Educating	Educat + ed/ing
Elevate	Elevated	Elevating	Elevat + ed/ing
Facilitate	Facilitated	Facilitating	Facilitat + ed/ing
Formulate	Formulated	Formulating	Formulat + ed/ing
Generate	Generated	Generating	Generat + ed/ing
Illustrate	Illustrated	Illustrating	Illustrat + ed/ing
Implement	Implemented	Implementing	Implement + ed/ing
Incorporate	Incorporated	Incorporating	Incorporat + ed/ing
Integrate	Integrated	Integrating	Integrat + ed/ing
Organize	Organized	Organizing	Organiz + ed/ing
Participate	Participated	Participating	Participat + ed/ing

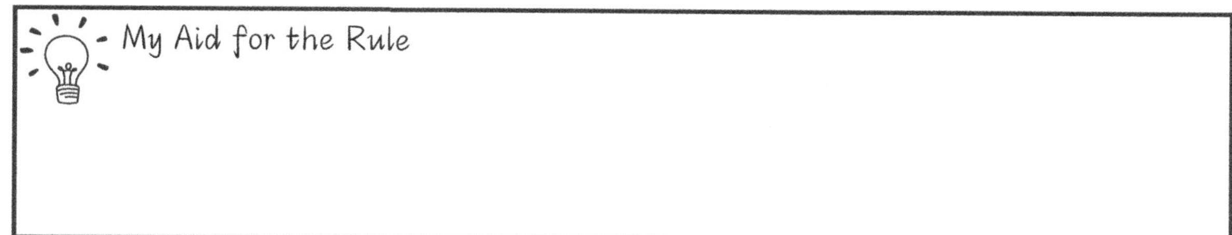 **Activity 30: Complete the paragraphs below by selecting the appropriate word from the provided list for each paragraph and adding the suffix *-ed* or *-ing* as needed to fit the context correctly.**

Collaborate Communicate Conclude Contribute

Delegate Demonstrate Facilitate Integrate

1. In their latest project, the team ________________________ effectively to achieve their goals. Each member ________________________ unique insights, while the leader ________________________ tasks strategically to ensure smooth progress. They ________________________ openly during meetings, which ________________________ better understanding and ________________________ everyone's efforts. By the end, they ________________________ the project successfully, with results that ________________________ their collective strength and commitment.

     SPELLING FOR ADULTS ©2025

Challenge Communicate Contribute Elevate Integrate Move

2. _________________________ to a new workplace can be _________________________, but collaborating with supportive colleagues makes the transition smoother. By _________________________ openly and participating actively in team projects, employees can quickly establish rapport. _________________________ into a new environment often requires adapting to existing workflows while _________________________ fresh ideas. With time, these efforts result in _________________________ both individual confidence and team performance.

Demonstrate Educate Elevate Encourage

Engage Generate Illustrate

3. The university professor _________________________ her students on critical thinking skills by _________________________ them to debate various perspectives. She ___________________ the value of evidence-based arguments and _________________________ key concepts with real-world examples. Her methods _________________________ enthusiasm for learning and formulated an ______________________ environment that _________________________ the students' understanding.

4. A local nonprofit has been _________________________________ the community about sustainability by _________________________________ its importance through interactive workshops. By demonstrating eco-friendly practices and _________________________________ cleanup events, they are actively _________________________________ to environmental awareness. Volunteers are participating in various initiatives, _________________________________ by the belief that small actions can lead to significant change over time.

Analyze Collaborate Communicate Conclude

Contribute Demonstrate Hope

5. The debate team moved through the regional rounds with confidence, _________________________________ to secure their spot at the national finals. They _________________________________ their opponents' arguments, calculating the strengths and weaknesses of each point. By _________________________________ during their preparation and _________________________________ effectively on stage, they _________________________________ a mastery of critical thinking and persuasion. As the final debate ended, they _________________________________ their presentation with a powerful statement, _________________________________ to a well-earned victory.

<u>Rule 6</u>

- When the base word ends with *ee*, *oe*, or *ye*, <u>keep</u> the final *e*.

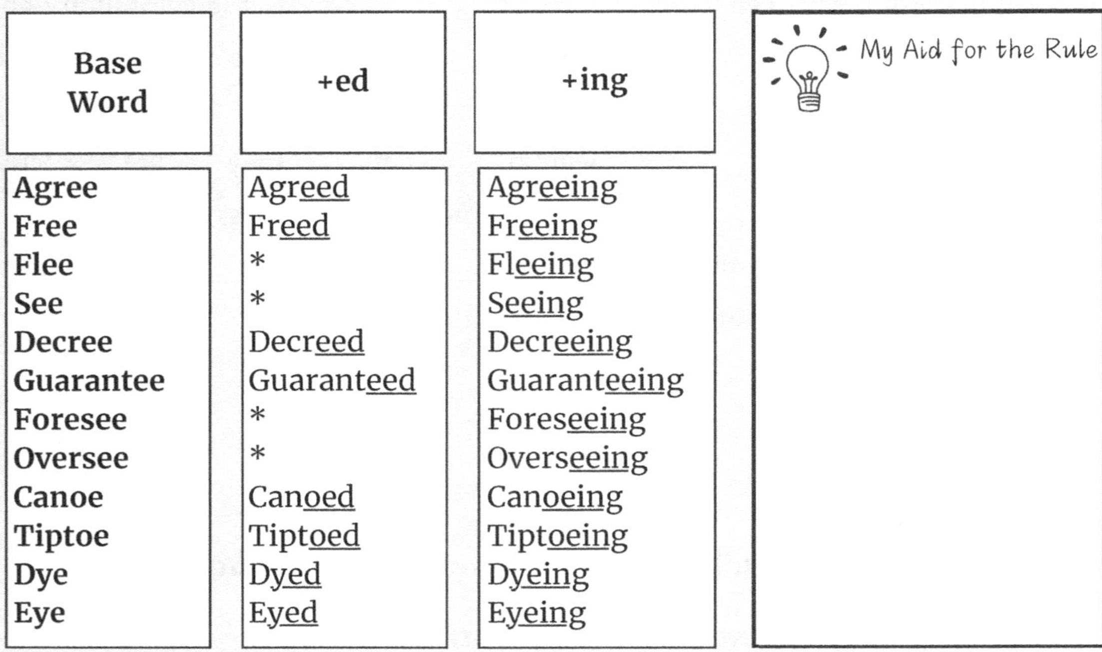

Base Word	+ed	+ing	 My Aid for the Rule
Agree	Agr<u>eed</u>	Agr<u>eeing</u>	
Free	Fr<u>eed</u>	Fr<u>eeing</u>	
Flee	*	Fl<u>eeing</u>	
See	*	S<u>eeing</u>	
Decree	Decr<u>eed</u>	Decr<u>eeing</u>	
Guarantee	Guarant<u>eed</u>	Guarant<u>eeing</u>	
Foresee	*	Fores<u>eeing</u>	
Oversee	*	Overs<u>eeing</u>	
Canoe	Can<u>oed</u>	Can<u>oeing</u>	
Tiptoe	Tipt<u>oed</u>	Tipt<u>oeing</u>	
Dye	Dy<u>ed</u>	Dy<u>eing</u>	
Eye	Ey<u>ed</u>	Ey<u>eing</u>	

*Irregular verb that does not take *-ed*.

Activity 31: Complete the paragraph below by selecting the appropriate suffixed word from the table above to fit the context correctly.

The council _____________________ to lift the village's curfew. To mark the momentous occasion, it was _____________________that a grand festival would be held, a celebration _____________________ to restore hope and unity among the villagers. As the preparations unfolded, children delighted in _____________________ past the dyers, _____________________ the vibrant pigments as they worked to create colorful banners and garments. Meanwhile, a team of adventurers set out on a _____________________ journey to the distant waterfall, to fetch rare flowers to decorate the festival grounds.

> **Does *y* change when adding *-ed* or *-ing*, and if so, when?**

Rule 7 and 8
- The letter *y* changes to *i* when adding the suffix *-ed*, if *y* follows a consonant.
- The letter *y* does not change to *i* when adding the suffix *-ing*.

Base Word ends in consonant + y	When adding *-ed*	When adding *-ing*
Cry	Cried	Crying
Carry	Carried	Carrying
Hurry	Hurried	Hurrying
Reply	Replied	Replying
Multiply	Multiplied	Multiplying
Apply	Applied	Applying
Comply	Complied	Complying
Deny	Denied	Denying
Simplify	Simplified	Simplifying
Verify	Verified	Verifying

<u>Rule 9:</u>

- **The letter _y_ stays the same regardless of the suffix being added when it follows a vowel.**

Base Word ends in vowel + y	When adding -ed	When adding -ing
Stay Enjoy Delay Convey Display	Stayed Enjoyed Delayed Conveyed Displayed	Staying Enjoying Delaying Conveying Displaying

My Aid for the Rules

 **Activity 32:** Add *-ed* and *-ing* to each base word in the table and write them in their respective columns. Apply rules 7-9 from this unit to ensure correct spelling. Use the *My Notes and Definitions* space provided for any notes or dictionary work as needed.

Base Word	+ -ed	+ -ing
Apply		
Betray		
Buy	---	
Clarify		
Classify		
Comply		
Convey		
Decay		

My Notes and Definitions

Base Word	+ -ed	+ -ing
Declassify		
Defy		
Delay		
Deny		
Deploy		
Display		
Disqualify		
Diversify		
Employ		
Enjoy		
Exemplify		
Falsify		

My Notes and Definitions

Base Word	+ -ed	+ -ing
Glorify		
Identify		
Justify		
Notify		
Obey		
Pacify		
Pay		
Play		
Portray		
Pray		
Purvey		
Quantify		

My Notes and Definitions

Base Word	**+ -ed**	**+ -ing**
Query		
Relay		
Say		
Simplify		
Spay		
Spy		
Stay		
Survey		
Sway		
Try		
Verify		
Worry		

My Notes and Definitions

 **Activity 33:** For each base word in the list provided below, decide whether to add *-ed* or *-ing* based on the context of the passage titled *Managing Personal Finances*. Then, fill in the blanks using the correct word form.

Note: This activity is split into sections to make it easier to focus on each part of the passage. Take your time to review the rules covered in this unit before starting. The word marked with an asterisk (*) is used twice in the passage.

Classify Juggle Organize Simplify Spend

Managing Personal Finances

Managing finances can feel overwhelming, especially when you're ______________________ multiple expenses, investments, and unexpected costs. However, ______________________ your financial plan can help you stay ______________________ and make smarter decisions. Here are some steps to consider, using real-life scenarios to illustrate how they work.

Step 1: Classify Your Expenses

Start by ______________________ your expenses into categories like housing, utilities, groceries, and discretionary ______________________.

The Rules at a Glance
When Adding *-ed* and *-ing*

Doubling the Final Consonant

1. 1 syllable + CVC → Double the final consonant.
2. Multi-syllable + CVC + stressed final syllable → Double the final consonant.
3. Do NOT double if:
   - The word does not meet Rule 1 or Rule 2.
   - The word ends with more than one consonant.

SPELLING FOR ADULTS ©2025

The Rules at a Glance
When Adding *-ed* and *-ing*

Silent *-e*
- Silent *-e* → Drop the *e* before adding vowel suffixes (*-ed* or *-ing*).
- Exceptions: Words ending in -ee, -oe, or -ye → Keep the final e.

Changing *y*
- Consonant + *y* → Change *y* to *i* before adding
  -ed (→ *ied*). Keep y for *-ing* (→ *ying*).
- Vowel + *y* → Keep the *y*.

Deploy Identify Notify Quantify

By doing so, you'll clearly see where your money is going. For example, Samantha, a single mother, recently _____________________ that 30% of her income was spent on dining out. By ______________________ her spending habits, she was able to cut back and save for her daughter's college fund.

Step 2: Deploy a Budget

Once you've sorted your expenses, the next step is _____________________ a budget. Samantha used a budgeting app that _____________________ her every time she approached her monthly limit in any category. Sticking to her plan required discipline, but the regular updates kept her accountable.

Step 3: Diversify Your Investments

Financial experts often recommend ___________________________ your investments to minimize risk. While Samantha focused on ___________________ off debt, her brother, Brandon, was trying to grow his wealth. He began by ___________________________ conservative with bonds before applying some funds toward stocks. When the stock market took a downturn, his ___________________________ portfolio helped him avoid significant losses.

Step 4: Pay Off Debt Strategically

Debt can feel insurmountable, but ___________________________ it strategically is key. For instance, many people struggle with credit card balances, which accumulate high interest over time. By ___________________________ the card with the highest interest rate and applying extra payments toward that balance, you can save money in the long run. Samantha, for example, tackled her debts one at a time, ___________________________ each payment as an investment in her future peace of mind.

Need a break? Head over to the Take a Break page for free fun crossword and word search puzzles created just for you. Scan the QR code or visit the link below to get started!

https://natashascripts.com/takeabreak-spelling-puzzles/

Step 5: Relay Information to Family

Financial ___________________________ often involves others, especially family members. Samantha realized she ___________________________ to relay her plans to her teenage son to teach him about budgeting early. This step exemplified her dedication to ___________________________ financial literacy within her household.

Step 6: Stay Vigilant Against Fraud

Another critical aspect of ___________________________ finances is staying alert for fraud. Scammers often use tactics like ___________________________ emails or spying on financial transactions to steal information. Samantha, for instance, received a suspicious email that ___________________________ itself as her bank. By verifying the sender's details with the bank directly, she avoided falling victim to a phishing scam.

Step 7: Enjoy Financial Freedom

Once you've taken control of your finances, it's important to pause and reflect on your progress. Samantha eventually reached a point where she could save for vacations and other luxuries, fully ___________________________ the rewards of her hard work. She even treated herself to a weekend getaway, using money she had intentionally set aside for relaxation.

Concluding Thoughts

Financial health requires effort, but by _________________________ these steps, you can pacify the stress and take control of your future. Whether it's through classifying, budgeting, or _____________________ vigilant, small actions can lead to significant results. Like Samantha, you'll soon find yourself in a place where you can both justify and enjoy your financial decisions with confidence.

Supplementary Practice Program for Adults

To reinforce what you've learned in this unit, download and print the corresponding worksheets by visiting the following webpage or scanning the QR code.

https://natashascripts.com/spelling-extra-practice-adults/

Unit 6: Spelling Words with Confusing Vowel Suffixes (*-ar, -er, -or, -ary, -ery, -ory*)

Introduction

This unit explores vowel suffixes that often confuse even the most skilled spellers, particularly when deciding whether a word ends in *-ar*, or *-er*, or *-ary*, or *-ory*. These suffixes don't follow absolute spelling rules; instead, they are shaped by conventions with exceptions. The lessons cover essential vocabulary ending in these suffixes, as well as terms commonly used in professional and academic contexts.

Unit Overview

The lessons in this unit focus on:
- Examining how vowel suffixes modify words
- Understanding the conventions and exceptions that govern these suffixes.
- Studying essential vocabulary used in professional and academic contexts.

To simplify learning, each suffix pattern is discussed separately and supported by visual aids and tables. You are encouraged to take your time and, if needed, break the lessons into smaller sections with short breaks.

By the end of this unit, you will be able to:
- **Decide which vowel suffix (*-ar*, *-er*, *-ary*, *-ery*, or *-ory*) is correct to add to a given word based on established conventions and contextual clues.**
- **Identify and apply the most important exceptions to these general patterns.**
- **Practice using these words in complete sentences to reinforce your understanding and proper application in context.**

Supplementary Practice Program

To further reinforce the lessons in this unit, you can download the corresponding supplementary worksheets designed for extra practice. The link and QR code to access these worksheets are provided at the end of this unit.

Lesson 20: Choosing the Right Suffix *-ar, -er, -or*

> **How do I know whether to use *-ar, -er,* or *-or* at the end of a word?**

The suffixes *-ar, -er,* and *-or* are pronounced similarly in words that end with them. Moreover, all three suffixes serve the same function in a word, which makes determining the correct one quite confusing. The suffixes are commonly used to **transform a verb into a noun**, specifically to describe a person, thing, or agent that performs an action (noun of agency). For example:

- *Teach* becomes ***teacher*** (a person who teaches).
- *Act* becomes ***actor*** (a person who acts).
- *Beg* becomes ***beggar*** (a person who begs).

There are patterns and practices in English that can guide you in choosing the correct suffix, but these are not strict rules, and exceptions must be studied and remembered.

Among the three suffixes, *-er* is by far the most commonly used, followed by *-or*, with *-ar* being the least common.

Why Start with *-or?*
We will begin with the patterns for the suffix *-or* because once you learn the word patterns that typically take *-or*, you can safely assume that most other words will take *-er*. As these are conventions and not hard-and-fast rules, there will be exceptions. These exceptions will also be listed so you can note them and study them as needed.

The Suffix *-or*

Use *-or* with the following word patterns:

1. Verbs ending in *-ct*
   - Example: abduct → abductor

2. Verbs ending in *-ate* which have more than one syllable
   - Example: calculate → calculator

3. Verbs ending in *-it* which have more than one syllable
   - Example: exhibit → exhibitor

4. Verbs ending in *-ise*
   - Example: supervise → supervisor

1. Verbs ending in *-ct*

abduct → abductor	correct → corrector	instruct → instructor
act → actor	construct → constructor	obstruct → obstructor
contract → contractor	direct → director	project → projector
conduct → conductor	deflect → deflector	react → reactor
connect → connector	eject → ejector	reflect → reflector
constrict → constrictor	extract → extractor	select → selector
contract → contractor		

The *-ct* pattern is one of the most reliable to follow, as it applies to most verbs ending in *-ct*, with very few significant exceptions. The list above provides a comprehensive collection of the most important verbs ending in *-ct* that take the suffix *-or* to form a noun.

2. Verbs ending in *-ate*
+
More than one Syllable

abbreviate → abbreviator   dictate → dictator
abdicate → abdicator   educate → educator
accelerate → accelerator   escalate → escalator
accept → acceptor   estimate → estimator
adjudicate → adjudicator   fabricate → fabricator
agitate → agitator   levitate → levitator
animate → animator   meditate → meditator
arbitrate → arbitrator   moderate → moderator
authenticate → authenticator   modulate → modulator
calibrate → calibrator   navigate → navigator

Note:

Verbs ending in *-ate* that have **one syllable only** will take the suffix *-er* :

E.g.,
- *grate → grater*
- *hate → hater*
- *skate → skater*

The *-ate* pattern, like the *-ct* pattern, is also highly reliable. Most multi-syllable verbs ending in *-ate* take *-or* to form a noun.

3. Verbs ending in -*it*
+
More than one syllable

inhibit → inhibitor	audit → auditor
inherit → inheritor	credit → creditor
solicit → solicitor	edit → editor
visit → visitor	elicit → elicitor

Exceptions:

babysit → babysitter	forfeit → forfeiter
delimit → delimiter	orbit → orbiter
emit → emitter	profit → profiter
exploit → exploiter	recruit → recruiter
	wait → waiter

Note:
Verbs ending in -*it* with **only one syllable** take the suffix -*er*, and the final *t* is usually doubled:

E.g.,
- *sit → sitter*
- *quit → quitter*
- *fit → fitter*

Although there are exceptions to this pattern, as noted in the exceptions section above, the most significant verbs ending in -*it* that take the suffix -*or* to form a noun are listed in the table above.

4. Verbs ending in -*ise*

Exception:
advertise → advertiser

advise → advisor
improvise → improvisor
incise → incisor
supervise → supervisor

In American English, very few verbs end with the suffix -*ise*, and even fewer take -*or* to form a noun. Most verbs ending in -*ise* are derived from Latin. Otherwise, the suffix -*ize* is the standard form in American English. It is important to note that when -*ize* verbs are transformed into nouns, they typically take the more common suffix -*er* (e.g., organize → organizer).

Need a break? *Head over to the Take a Break page for free fun crossword and word search puzzles created just for you. Scan the QR code or visit the link below to get started!*

https://natashascripts.com/takeabreak-spelling-puzzles/

SPELLING FOR ADULTS ©2025

 **Activity 34:** Answer each question in a full sentence, using the bolded *-or* noun in your response. Typical answers are provided in the answer key.

1. What does an **abductor** do, and why is this word often associated with criminal activity?

____

____

2. Why might a **contractor** be hired, and what types of projects might they work on?

____

____

3. What kind of animal is a **constrictor**, and how does it capture its prey?

____

____

4. What is a color **corrector**, and how is it used in visual media or makeup?

____

____

5. What is the role of a **director**, and in what fields might they work?

____

____

6. What does an **extractor** do?

____

____

7. What does an **instructor** do and in what fields might they work?

____

____

Now that you know the patterns for -*or*, it will be easier to determine whether a verb takes -*er* when forming its noun. This is because most verbs that do not follow the patterns for -*or*, as previously discussed, will almost always take the suffix -*er*.

To simplify the process further, we will now discuss some common patterns for -*er* as well.

Use -*er* with the following word patterns:

1. Verbs ending in a single vowel followed by a single consonant
   - Example: read → reader

2. Verbs ending in two or more consonants, except -*ct*
   - Example: contend → contender
       - golf → golfer
       - tempt → tempter
       - watch → watcher

3. Verbs ending in a double consonant, except -*ss*
   - Example: call → caller
       - sniff → sniffer

4. Verbs ending in a silent -*e*
   - Example: give → giver

     SPELLING FOR ADULTS ©2025

<table>
<tr><td>

1. Verbs ending in Vowel + Consonant

</td><td>

box → boxer
cater → caterer
flip → flipper
format → formatter
garden → gardener
jog → jogger
lead → leader
log → logger

</td><td>

plaster → plasterer
program → programmer
propel → propeller
shred → shredder
swim → swimmer
train → trainer
travel → traveler
win → winner

</td></tr>
</table>

Exceptions:
conquer → conqueror
counsel → counselor
council → councillor
jail → jailor
offer → offeror
sail → sailor
transfer → transferor

Note:
The rules for doubling final consonants when adding vowel suffixes apply here. To review these rules, refer to Unit 5.

---

2. Verbs ending in two or more consonants except –*ct*

Exceptions:
invent → inventor
invest → investor
sculpt → sculptor
torment → tormentor
vend → vendor

Note:
Verbs ending in –*ct* usually take the suffix –*or*.

–*ld*
build → builder
hold → holder
mold → molder
shield → shielder
yield → yielder
weld → welder

–*nd*
blend → blender
command → commander
compound → compounder
contend → contender
impound → impounder
pretend → pretender
remind → reminder
respond → responder

–*lf*
golf → golfer

–*pt*
adapt → adapter
adopt → adopter
disrupt → disrupter
interrupt → interrupter
prompt → prompter

–*rt*
convert → converter
export → exporter
report → reporter
transport → transporter

–*st*
defrost → defroster
dust → duster
forest → forester
harvest → harvester
protest → protester

-ch	*-tch*	*-sh*
crunch → cruncher	catch → catcher	demolish → demolisher
preach → preacher	dispatch → dispatcher	extinguish → extinguisher
research → researcher	etch etcher	refurbish → refurbisher
teach → teacher	sketch → sketcher	polish → polisher
march → marcher	snatch → snatcher	publish → publisher
	watch → watcher	refresh → refresher
		wash → washer

3. Verbs ending in a double consonant, except -ss

-ff	*-ll*	*-zz*
bluff → bluffer	call → caller	buzz → buzzer
puff → puffer	distill → distiller	
scoff → scoffer	fill → filler	
sniff → sniffer	mill → miller	
stuff → stuffer	roll → roller	
	sell → seller	
	spell → speller	

Note:
Verbs ending in -ss may take either -er or -or, with **no fixed pattern to follow**.

Verbs ending in -ss that take -er when forming a noun:
- address → addresser
- amass → amasser
- guess → guesser
- harass → harasser
- hiss → hisser
- kiss → kisser
- repress → represser
- trespass → trespasser

Verbs ending in -ss that take -or when forming a noun:
- assess → assessor
- compress → compressor
- confess → confessor
- depress → depressor
- dispossess → dispossessor
- oppress → oppressor
- possess → possessor
- process → processor
- stress → stressor
- suppress → suppressor
- transgress → transgressor

SPELLING FOR ADULTS ©2025

<table>
<tr><td>4. Verbs ending in a silent -e</td><td>dance → dancer
compose → composer
examine → examiner
game → gamer
hike → hiker
lecture → lecturer
manage → manager

observe → observer
produce → producer
receive → receiver
trade → trader
weave → weaver
write → writer</td></tr>
</table>

Note:
Verbs ending in -*ise*, which contain a silent -*e*, do not fall into this category, but usually take the suffix -*or*.

The Suffix -*ar*

Like -*er* and -*or*, the suffix -*ar* can also form nouns from verbs. However, this usage is rare, as very few verbs take -*ar* to form a noun.

It is important to note that while -*ar* is uncommon as a noun-forming suffix, it frequently appears in adjectives, such as *spectacular, regular,* and *ocular.* In these cases, -*ar* is not functioning as a suffix because it is not modifying a base word to create a new word with a different grammatical function.

There is no set pattern to determine whether a verb takes the suffix -*ar* to form a noun. However, only two verbs follow this pattern: ***beg → beggar*** and ***lie → liar***.

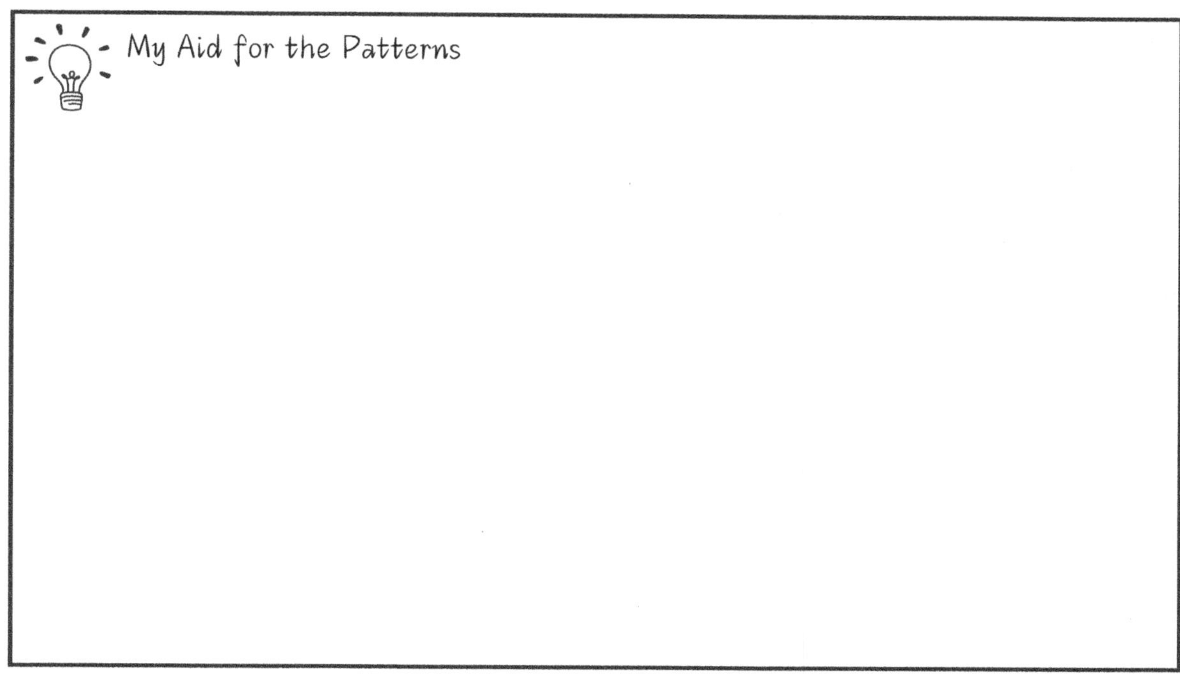

Activity 35: Transform each verb into a noun by adding the correct suffix (*-er*, *-or*, or *-ar*). Write the complete noun form next to each verb.

Examine ___________________

Contract ___________________

Beg ___________________

Supervise ___________________

Agitate ___________________

Instruct ___________________

Protest ___________________

Correct ___________________

Receive ___________________

Format ___________________

Accelerate ___________________

Sketch ___________________

Propel ___________________

Log ___________________

SPELLING FOR ADULTS ©2025

Transgress	_____________		Oppress	_____________
Educate	_____________		Spell	_____________
Inhibit	_____________		Quit	_____________
Advise	_____________		Travel	_____________
Program	_____________		Contend	_____________
Process	_____________		Trespass	_____________
Research	_____________		Distill	_____________
Modulate	_____________		Kiss	_____________
Audit	_____________		Obstruct	_____________
Adapt	_____________		Incise	_____________

 **Activity 36: Read each definition and choose the correctly spelled word that matches the given definition.**

1. A person who judges or makes official decisions in disputes or competitions.
A. adjudicater
B. adjudicator

2. A person or authority who seizes and holds property, animals, or vehicles by legal authority.
A. impounder
B. impoundor

3. A person who evaluates or determines the value, quality, or level of something, often in finance or education.
A. assesser
B. assessor

4. A person who calculates or approximates the cost, value, or amount of something, especially in construction or business.
A. estimater
B. estimator

5. A person or thing that interrupts, disturbs, or causes disorder, often in a system or industry.
A. disrupter
B. disruptor

6. A person who observes or monitors something carefully, such as a security guard or spectator.
A. watcher
B. watchor

7. A person who restrains, suppresses, or controls actions, emotions, or movements, often by force.
A. represser
B. repressor

8. A person who mixes or combines substances, especially in medicine or chemistry.
A. compounder
B. compoundor

9. A lawyer who advises clients, prepares legal documents, and may represent them in court.
A. soliciter
B. solicitor

10. A device or person that puts out fires or stops something from continuing.
A. extinguisher
B. extinguishor

11. A person or device that prevents or reduces the force, activity, or expression of something.
A. suppresser
B. suppressor

12. A person who admits to wrongdoing or listens to confessions, often in a religious or legal context.
A. confesser
B. confessor

13. A person who makes a formal proposal or offer, especially in legal or business transactions.
A. offerer
B. offeror

 **Activity 37: Read each passage carefully. Some words are spelled incorrectly because they have the wrong suffix. Identify and correct each error by writing the correctly spelled word in the Corrections Box.**

1. A Legal Dispute

The adjudicater listened carefully as both sides presented their arguments. The soliciter representing the company insisted that the evidence was sufficient, while the defense argued otherwise. The assessor was called in to evaluate the financial damage. In the end, the offerer decided to settle the case outside of court.

Corrections Box

2. Safety at the Factory

The factory had several safety measures in place, including a fire extinguisher in every room. Workers were reminded that the impoundor would remove any unauthorized items from workstations. The compoundar in the chemical department carefully mixed substances, while the watchor monitored surveillance cameras to ensure security.

Corrections Box

3. Work on a Farm

The farm relied on a skilled irrigater to ensure crops received enough water. The transportar loaded fresh produce onto trucks to be delivered to markets across the region. A compounder worked in the processing plant, mixing different types of fertilizers to enhance soil quality. Meanwhile, a selecter carefully picked the ripest fruits for packaging. In the evening, the farm's supervisor checked the workers' progress and made sure everything was running efficiently.

Corrections Box

4. Charity Gala

The local shelter was grateful to the adoptar who took in three rescued dogs. A well-known motivater was invited to give an inspiring talk to encourage more people to volunteer. At the fundraising event, a narrator shared stories of families who had been helped by the organization. The organizers also hired an auctioneer to run the charity auction smoothly. Meanwhile, a collecter went around gathering donations from attendees. The evening ended with a heartfelt message from the directer, who expressed deep appreciation for everyone's generosity.

Corrections Box

Understanding the function of a word is essential. In the previous lesson, we explored how verbs can be transformed into nouns by adding the suffixes -*er*, -*or*, and -*ar*. In this lesson, we will focus on adjectives that end in -*ar*.

Now that you know -*ar* is not a common noun-forming suffix, it's important to recognize that many words ending in -*ar* are actually adjectives. Studying these words will help reduce uncertainty when spelling words that contain the *ar/er/or* sound.

This lesson will focus on frequently used words in everyday writing, the workplace, and academic contexts.

Many words ending in *ar* are **adjectives. Adjectives describe or modify nouns by giving more information about their quality, quantity, or state.**

Examples:
1. The debate over <u>nuclear</u> energy continues, with some arguing for its efficiency and others concerned about its risks.
- *Nuclear* (adjective) describes the type of **energy** (noun).

2. Unlike religious institutions, <u>secular</u> organizations do not follow any religious principles in their operations.
- *Secular* (adjective) describes the type of **organizations** that operate without religious affiliation.

3. His <u>particular</u> approach to problem-solving made him an invaluable team member.
- *Particular* (adjective) describes the **specific nature of his approach** to solving problems.

Activity 38: The words in the list are adjectives that describe a noun (bolded) within the sentence. Choose the correct adjective that best fits the context of each sentence below.

Circular Molecular Nuclear Ocular Particular Perpendicular

Popular Secular Spectacular Vascular

1. The scientist conducted _____________________ **research** to analyze how atoms interact at a microscopic level.

2. The professor emphasized the importance of using _____________________ **reasoning** rather than jumping to conclusions.

3. The _____________________ **design** of the conference hall allows for better acoustics.

4. The _____________________ **event** attracted thousands of people and was a huge success.

5. The hospital specializes in treating _____________________ **disorders** related to blood circulation.

6. The telescope provided a clearer view of celestial objects, enhancing _____________________ **observations**.

7. Unlike religious schools, public education systems follow a _____________________ **curriculum**.

8. The new **café** quickly became _____________________ among students because of its relaxed atmosphere and great coffee.

9. Engineers designed **the bridge's supports** to be perfectly _____________________ to the ground for stability.

10. The _____________________ energy **plant** generates power for the entire city.

 **Activity 39: Match each *-ar* adjective to its correct definition. Write the corresponding word next to each definition.**

Bipolar   Cardiovascular   Granular   Linear   Lunar

Radicular   Solar   Tabular   Triangular   Vernacular

1. Arranged in a straight line   ________________________

2. Relating to the sun   ____________________

3. Having a shape with three sides   ____________________

4. Affecting the heart and blood vessels   ____________________

5. Having two opposite extremes   ____________________

6. Relating to the moon   ____________________

7. Consisting of small particles   ____________________

8. Relating to everyday speech or informal language   ____________________

9. Referring to a structured table format   ____________________

10. Relating to roots or nerve roots   ____________________

Dictionary Work

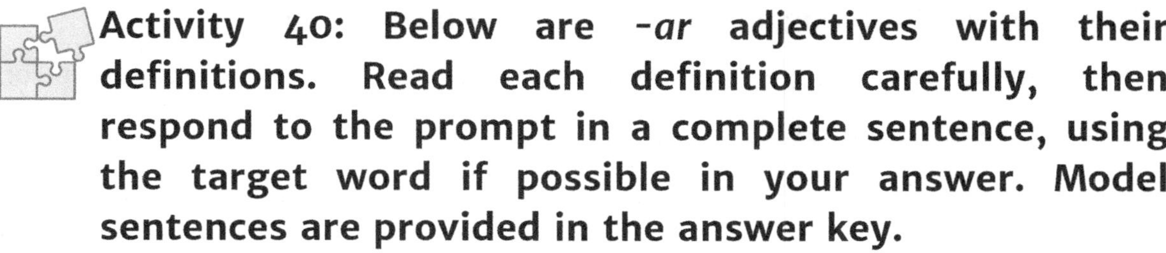

Activity 40: Below are -ar adjectives with their definitions. Read each definition carefully, then respond to the prompt in a complete sentence, using the target word if possible in your answer. Model sentences are provided in the answer key.

1. Cellular: Relating to cells or a network of small units.

- Describe how cellular technology has improved communication in your daily life or workplace.

____

____

____

2. Granular: Made up of small particles; detailed or highly specific.

- Explain why having a granular understanding of a project or budget is important in professional settings.

____

____

____

3. Insular: Isolated or narrow-minded, often referring to communities or perspectives.

- Describe a situation where an insular mindset prevented progress in a workplace or social setting.

____

____

____

          SPELLING FOR ADULTS ©2025

4. Irregular: Not following a pattern; uneven or inconsistent.

- Talk about a challenge you faced due to irregular work schedules or unpredictable deadlines.

____

____

____

5. Singular: Unique, extraordinary, or referring to a single item.

- Write about a singular achievement or experience that made a significant impact on your life.

____

____

____

6. Collateral: Secondary or related but not primary; also refers to loan security.

- In what situations might collateral damage happen, even when it's unintended?

____

____

____

7. Polar: Extremely opposite or related to the Earth's poles.

- Talk about two polar opinions you have encountered in a debate or discussion.

____

____

____

 **Activity 41: Each of the words below is used in a short, incomplete sentence. Expand each sentence by adding at least 8 more words to create a meaningful and detailed statement. Model answers are provided in the answer key.**

Example:
- **Original**: The concert was spectacular.
- **Expanded**: The concert was spectacular **because the stage lighting, live band, and fireworks made it an unforgettable experience.**

1. His schedule is very regular. _______________________________________

____

2. That face looks familiar to me. _______________________________________

____

3. The policy was unpopular among employees. _______________________

____

4. She has a particular way of organizing her work. _________________

____

5. The sunset over the mountains was spectacular. _________________

____

          SPELLING FOR ADULTS ©2025

> ## When should I use *-ary*, *-ery*, or *-ory* at the end of a word?

Words ending in *-ary, -ery,* and *-ory* are mostly derived from Old or Late Latin, often entering modern English through Old French or Middle English, which had borrowed them from Latin.

There are no absolute rules that dictate when a word ending with the "ary" sound takes *-ary, -ery,* or *-ory.* However, there are patterns and conventions that can serve as helpful guidelines.

1. Words Ending in *-ary*
- **Pattern: The root word cannot stand alone as an independent word when *-ary* is removed.**
  - If the root is incomplete or does not function as a standalone noun or verb, it probably takes *-ary.*
    - **Tip**: Ask yourself, "Does the root word stand alone or make sense on its own?" If the answer is **no**, then it is probably spelled with *-ary* at the end.

Target Word	Root Word	Does it make sense on its own?
Adversary	Advers-	x
Arbitrary	Arbitr-	x
Anniversary	Annivers-	x
Culinary	Culin-	x
Centenary	Centen-	x
Contrary	Contr-	x
Extraordinary	Extraordin-	x
Involuntary	Involunt-	x

Words that do not follow this pattern: *complementary (complement), fragmentary (fragment), illusionary (illusion), sugary (sugar), supplementary (supplement).*

2. Words Ending in *-ery*

- Pattern: The base word exists as a noun, verb, or adjective before adding *-ery*.
  - If the base word already has a grammatical function, particularly as a noun, verb, or adjective, it probably takes *-ery*.
    - **Tip**: Ask yourself, "Does the base word already exist as a noun, verb, or adjective?" If **yes**, then it probably takes *-ery*.

Target Word	Base Word	Base Word Function
Bakery	Bake	Verb
Bravery	Brave	Adjective
Bribery	Bribe	Noun, Verb
Distillery	Distill	Verb
Eatery	Eat	Verb
Fishery	Fish	Noun, Verb
Forgery	Forge	Verb
Imagery	Image	Noun
Winery	Wine	Noun
Slavery	Slave	Noun
Scenery	Scene	Noun
Recovery	Recover	Verb
Robbery	Robber	Noun
Delivery	Deliver	Verb
Powdery	Powder	Noun, Verb
Mastery	Master	Noun, Verb

Words that do not follow this pattern: *adultery, archery, artery, artillery, battery, celery, cemetery, surgery, fiery, gallery, lottery, misery, monastery, mystery, query.*

     SPELLING FOR ADULTS ©2025

3. Words Ending in *-ory*

- Pattern: The root word cannot stand alone, but a related verb (or sometimes noun) can be identified by adding a silent *-e* or modifying the last letter(s), or adding *-ate*.
  - Many verbs ending in *-ate, -t* and *-s*, take *-ory* when transformed into a noun.
    - Tip – Ask yourself, "Can I identify a related verb or noun by adding a silent *-e* (or *-ate*) or slightly modifying the root?" If yes, then the word probably takes *-ory*.

	Identifying a related
Target Word	**verb or noun**
Accessory	*Access* – Verb, Noun
Acclamatory	**Acclaim** – Verb
Advisory	**Advise** – Verb
Celebratory	**Celebrate** – Verb
Compensatory	**Compensate** – Verb
Declaratory	**Declare** – Verb
Derogatory	**Derogate** – Verb
Inflammatory	**Inflame** – Verb
Inventory	**Invent** – Verb
Introductory	**Introduce** – Verb

Words that do not follow this pattern: *compulsory, factory, story, category, hickory, history, ivory, laboratory, inventory, memory, premonitory, savory, theory, victory.*

The Patterns at a Glance:

- *-Ary* → The root word does not stand alone as a complete word.

- *-Ery* → The base word is a noun, verb, or adjective and exists independently.

- *-Ory* → The base word does not stand alone, but if slightly modified, a related verb can be identified.

Note: Remember that these are patterns to help guide you generally. They are not strict rules and are subject to exceptions.

Activity 42: Fill in the blanks with the correct suffix (*-ary, -ery, or -ory*) to complete each word. Use what you've learned about base words and patterns to determine the correct spelling. Refer to the quick guide above if you're unsure.

Culin________	Rudiment________	Rosem________
Advers________	Precaution________	Sal________
Ancill________	Prelimin________	Sanctu________
Annivers________	Prim________	Burgl________
Arbitr________	Pulmon________	Complement________
Evolution________	Respirat________	Brib________
Itiner________	Regulat________	Brew________
Machin________	Revis________	Brav________
Imag________	Satisfact________	Mock________
Forg________	Sens________	Mast________
Glitt________	Flow________	Adjudicat________

Fish________

Eat________

Drap________

Brok________

Distill________

Reaction________

Salut________

Sanit________

Sug________

Terti________

Derogat________

Depilat________

Defamat________

Declarat________

Corroborat________

Scen________

Auxili________

Caution________

Contr________

Diet________

Extraordin________

Statut________

Transit________

Interrogat________

Investigat________

Invent________

Illus________

Not________

Secret________

Nurs________

Perfum________

Powd________

Deliv________

Recov________

Refin________

Robb________

Savag________

Collaborat________

Contribut________

Conservat________

Conciliat________

Compuls________

Anticipat________

Accusat________

Compensat________

Audit________

Slav________

Orang________

<table>
<tr><td>Words to Practice Further</td></tr>
</table>

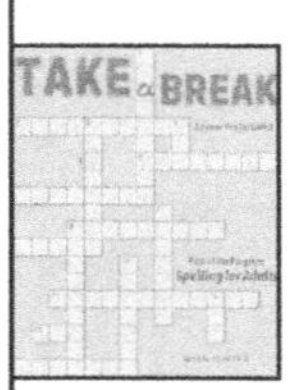

Need a break? *Head over to the Take a Break page for free fun crossword and word search puzzles created just for you. Scan the QR code or visit the link below to get started!*

https://natashascripts.com/takeabreak-spelling-puzzles/

Activity 43: Read each definition carefully and choose the correctly spelled word from the three options.

1. A question or inquiry.

a) Quary

b) Query

c) Quory

2. Basic or elementary in nature; relating to first principles.

a) Rudimentary

b) Rudimentery

c) Rudimentory

3. Based on random choice rather than reason.

a) Arbitrory

b) Arbitrery

c) Arbitrary

4. Ridicule or contemptuous behavior.

a) Mockary

b) Mockory

c) Mockery

5. Related to the movement of blood through the body.

a) Circulatary

b) Circulatory

c) Circulatery

6. Expressing or implying blame or wrongdoing.

a) Accusatary

b) Accusatery

c) Accusatory

7. A place of refuge or safety.

a) Sanctuary

b) Sanctuery

c) Sanctuory

8. Large-caliber weapons used in warfare.

a) Artillory

b) Artillery

c) Artillary

9. The process of regaining health or something lost.

a) Recovary

b) Recovery

c) Recovory

10. Intended to pacify or make peace.

a) Conciliatary

b) Conciliatery

c) Conciliatory

11. Offering money or gifts in exchange for favors or influence.

a) Bribery

b) Bribary

c) Bribory

12. Providing confirmation or support for something.

a) Corroboratary

b) Corroboratery

c) Corroboratory

13. A place where plants are grown or a school for artistic training.

a) Conservatary

b) Conservatory

c) Conservatery

14. Producing a beneficial or positive effect.

a) Salutary

b) Salutery

c) Salutory

15. The act of producing or using a fake document, signature, or work.

a) Forgery

b) Forgary

c) Forgory

16. A planned route or travel schedule.

a) Itinerary

b) Itinerery

c) Itinerory

17. An additional item used to complete or enhance something.

a) Accessary

b) Accessery

c) Accessory

18. A 100-year anniversary.

a) Centenary

b) Centenory

c) Centenery

19. Relating to hearing or sound.

a) Auditory

b) Auditary

c) Auditery

20. Providing additional support or help.

a) Auxiliary

b) Auxiliery

c) Auxiliory

21. Subordinate or supplementary in nature.

a) Ancillery

b) Ancillary

c) Ancillory

22. Expressing or implying blame or wrongdoing.

a) Accusatary

b) Accusatery

c) Accusatory

23. Required or enforced by rule or law.

a) Compulsary

b) Compulsory

c) Compulsery

24. Expressing expectation or preparation for something in the future.

a) Anticipatary

b) Anticipatery

c) Anticipatory

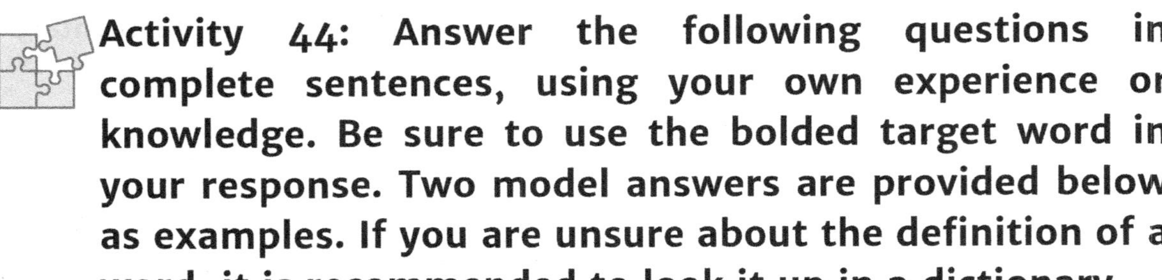

Activity 44: Answer the following questions in complete sentences, using your own experience or knowledge. Be sure to use the bolded target word in your response. Two model answers are provided below as examples. If you are unsure about the definition of a word, it is recommended to look it up in a dictionary.

Question 1: Have you ever had to follow an **arbitrary** rule that didn't seem to make sense? How did you feel about it?

Model Answer: At my previous job, we had an arbitrary rule that employees could not drink coffee at their desks, even though water and tea were allowed. No one understood the reason for it, and it made mornings difficult for coffee drinkers. Eventually, the rule was removed after employees complained.

Question 2: Think of a book, movie, or advertisement that used powerful **imagery**. How did it help convey the message?

Model Answer: One of my favorite books, *The Great Gatsby*, uses powerful imagery to describe wealth and excess during the 1920s. The author's descriptions of lavish parties, golden decorations, and shimmering lights helped me visualize the glamorous yet empty world the characters lived in.

3. What is an example of an **ancillary** service that makes your work or daily life easier?

____

____

____

4. When planning a trip, how do you create your **itinerary**, and what do you include in it?

____

____

____

5. Before making an important decision, what **preliminary** steps do you usually take?

____

____

____

6. What kind of **machinery** do you rely on in your job or home? How does it help you?

____

____

____

7. Have you ever submitted a **query** to customer service or a company? What was the issue?

____

____

____

8. Have you ever visited a **perfumery** or bought a fragrance from one? What was the experience like?

____

____

____

9. Can you think of an example where you took **anticipatory** action to prepare for an event or challenge?

____

____

____

10. What are some **compulsory** rules or regulations in your workplace or community?

____

____

____

11. What are some **regulatory** measures that help ensure safety in your country or workplace?

____

____

____

Note: Since responses will vary based on personal experiences, there are no answers in the answer key for this activity.

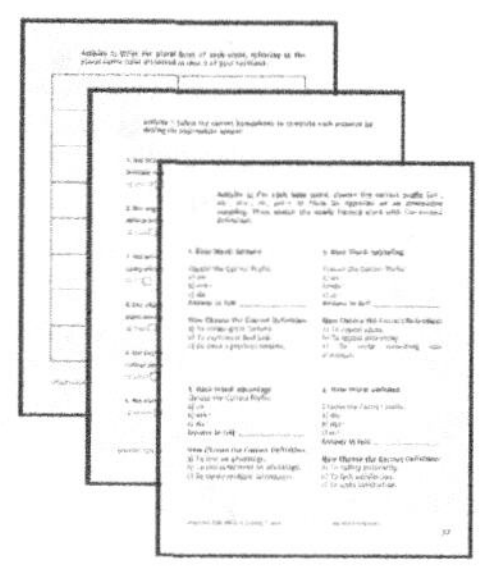

To reinforce what you've learned in this unit, download and print the corresponding worksheets by visiting the following webpage or scanning the QR code.

https://natashascripts.com/spelling-extra-practice-adults/

SPELLING FOR ADULTS ©2025

Unit 7: Spelling Patterns Through Phonograms

Introduction.
In this unit, we shift our focus to the sound side of spelling by studying phonograms—building blocks that connect letters with their sounds. Derived from the Greek *phono* (sound) and *gram* (character or symbol), phonograms reveal how letters work together to form the sounds of words. This perspective is especially important in English, where the names of letters often don't guide us accurately about the actual sounds they make, and where a single letter can produce multiple sounds.

Unit Overview
In the lessons of this unit, we will explore the soft and hard sounds produced by the letters *c* and *g*, and explain why these letters are pronounced hard, as in *cut* or *gum*, and soft, as in *cycle* or *gym*. Mastering the spelling patterns that determine these pronunciations is crucial, as many important English words rely on these conventions—a connection that can be traced back to their Latin origins. We will also study other phonograms derived from Old English, including *au, aw, ou, ow, ough*, and *augh*, and address the often confusing rules governing *ie* and *ei*. By examining these phonograms through clear explanations, visual aids, and tables, you will learn to decode words from their sound patterns rather than relying solely on letter names.

By the end of this unit, you will be able to:
- **Recognize and apply the spelling patterns associated with key phonograms.**
- **Determine the correct spelling when adding both vowel and consonant suffixes to base words that incorporate key phonograms.**
- **Accurately spell professional and academic vocabulary that contains key phonograms.**

Supplementary Practice Program
To further reinforce the lessons in this unit, you can download the corresponding supplementary worksheets designed for extra practice. The link and QR code to access these worksheets are provided at the end of this unit.

Lesson 23: The Soft and Hard Sounds of *c*

In English, the letter **c** can be pronounced soft, as in *ceiling*, or hard, as in *coffee*. There are fairly consistent rules that determine when *c* is pronounced one way or the other. These rules originated in Late Latin, carried over into French, and later influenced Middle English. The pronunciation of *c* usually depends on the letter that follows it each creating a phonogram, e.g. *ce, ci, cy*.

<u>Rule 1</u>
The letter *c* is pronounced like **s** when followed by the vowels **e, i, or y** in a word. This rule applies in most cases, with only a few exceptions.

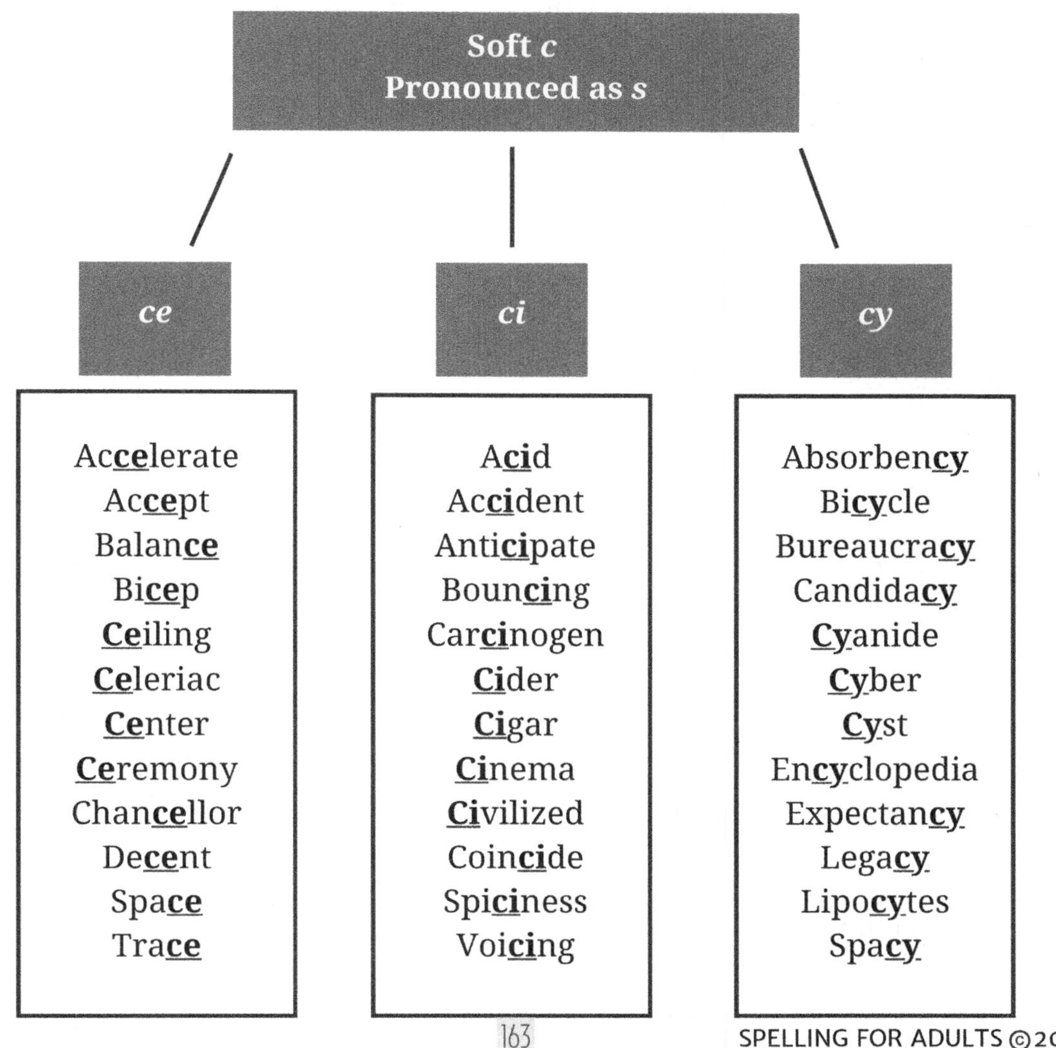

SPELLING FOR ADULTS ©2025

<u>Rule 2</u>
The letter *c* sounds like *k* before **a, o, or u**, as well as **before consonants** or **at the end of a word.**

Hard *c* pronounced as *k*

ca — A<u>ca</u>demy, Appli<u>ca</u>nt, <u>Ca</u>bin, <u>Ca</u>tegory, Logi<u>ca</u>l, S<u>ca</u>tter.

co — Ac<u>co</u>rd, A<u>co</u>rn, Ba<u>co</u>n, <u>Co</u>mpany, <u>Co</u>nverse, Teles<u>co</u>pe.

cu — Ac<u>cu</u>mulate, <u>Cu</u>lture, Se<u>cu</u>re, S<u>cu</u>lpture, Verna<u>cu</u>lar.

C + consonant — <u>Cl</u>imate, Un<u>cl</u>e, <u>Cr</u>ater, S<u>cr</u>ibble, Subtra<u>ct</u>, Ki<u>ck</u>.

C at the end of a word — Academi<u>c</u>, Anti<u>c</u>, Ar<u>c</u>, Pani<u>c</u>, Chroni<u>c</u>.

💡 My Aid for the Rules

1. Which letters after *c* make it sound like *s*?

2. Which letters after *c* make it sound like *k*?

 **Activity 45: Determine whether the underlined *c* in each word is pronounced with a hard or soft sound, by following the established rules.**

C	Hard	Soft
Ac<u>c</u>urate		
Relu<u>c</u>tant		
Voi<u>c</u>eover		
<u>C</u>ircuit		
Barri<u>c</u>ade		
Re<u>c</u>urring		
Autocra<u>c</u>y		
Tri<u>c</u>ycles		
Ac<u>c</u>use		
Bureau<u>c</u>rat		

C	**Hard**	**Soft**
Con**c**ern		
Civilized		
Ac**c**entuate		
Toxi**c**ology		
Sacrifi**c**e		
Crypto		
Carrier		
Centenary		
Bra**c**kets		
Ex**c**eption		
Corporate		
Academi**c**		

Lesson 24: The Soft and Hard Sounds of *g*

In the previous lesson, we explored the rules that determine when *c* is pronounced as soft or hard. **The same general pattern applies to *g*, but with more exceptions.**

Unlike *c*, which follows the soft/hard rule fairly consistently, *g* is less predictable. While the letter *g* is typically soft (as in *advantage*) when followed by *e, i,* or *y*, this rule has many exceptions. Some words containing *ge, gi,* or *gy* retain a hard *g* sound, as in *anger, begin,* and *gynecologist.*

Because of these exceptions, learning the patterns and common exceptions for *g* is essential for spelling and pronunciation accuracy.

Rule 1
The letter *g* is pronounced like *j* when followed by the vowels *e, i,* or *y* in a word. This rule applies in many cases, but there are also various **exceptions**.

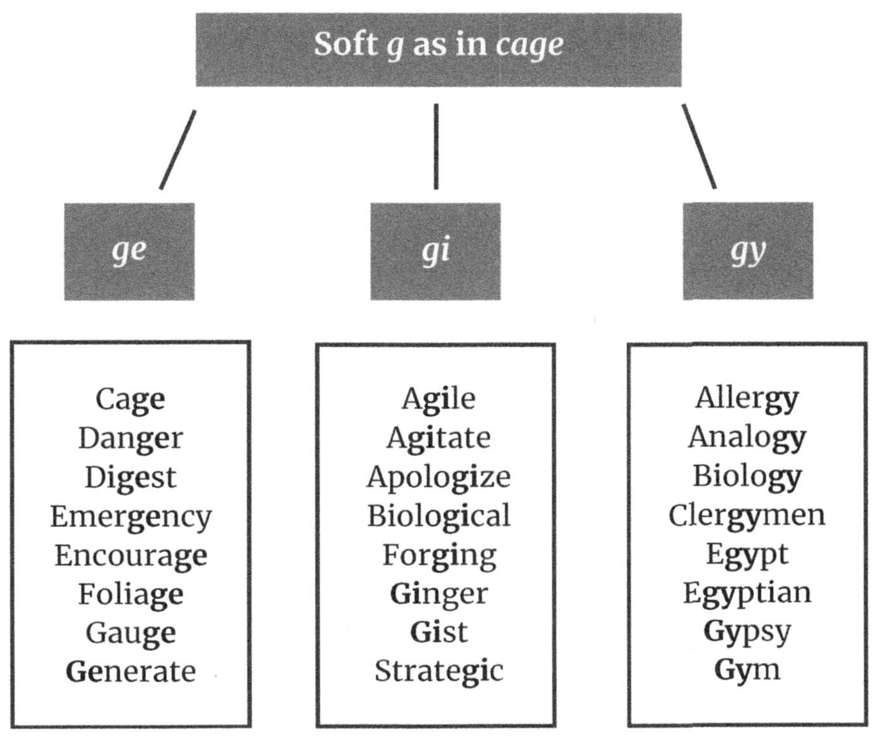

SPELLING FOR ADULTS ©2025

<u>Rule 2</u>
The letter *g* has a hard sound (as in *g*ap) before *a, o, or u*, as well as **before consonants** or **at the end of a word.**

Hard *g* as in *gap*

ga   Disreg<u>a</u>rd, <u>Ga</u>me, Org<u>a</u>nize, Eng<u>a</u>ge, Frug<u>a</u>l, <u>Ga</u>laxy.

go   Alg<u>o</u>rithm, Antag<u>o</u>nize, Categ<u>o</u>rize, Carg<u>o</u>, Vig<u>o</u>rous.

gu   Ambig<u>u</u>ous, Ang<u>u</u>lar, Biling<u>u</u>al, Fig<u>u</u>re, <u>Gu</u>idance, Reg<u>u</u>lar.

G + consonant   <u>Gl</u>amarous, Cong<u>l</u>omerate, <u>Gr</u>and, Agg<u>r</u>avate, Mag<u>n</u>et.

G at the end of a word   Absorbing, Among, Analog, Bag, Egg, Leg, Mug.

When *g* appears at the end of a word, it is usually doubled before adding the suffix *-ed* or *-ing*.

	Adding *-ed*	Adding *-ing*
Hug	Hugged	Hugging
Beg	Begged	Begging
Blog	Blogged	Blogging
Brag	Bragged	Bragging
Bug	Bugged	Bugging
Clog	Clogged	Clogging
Flag	Flagged	Flagging
Flog	Flogged	Flogging
Jog	Jogged	Jogging
Rig	Rigged	Rigging
Sag	Sagged	Sagging

 My Aid for the Rules

1. Which letters after *g* give it a soft sound?

2. Which letters after *g* give it a hard sound?

3. When is *g* doubled?

SPELLING FOR ADULTS ©2025

The Phonograms *gui* and *gue*

Words with the phonograms **gui** and **gue** are usually derived from French and Spanish. In these words, *u* is inserted to ensure that *g* is pronounced hard, as in *guerilla, argue, plague, guitar, colleague, fatigue,* and *epilogue.*

Some words that follow the same pattern but are not derived from French or Spanish include *guess* and *tongue.* These two words originate from Old English.

The Phonogram *gh*

The phonogram **gh** in certain English words comes from borrowed Italian words. The silent *h* is inserted to ensure a hard *g* sound before *e*, which would otherwise be pronounced soft. Examples include *spaghetti, Margherita, ghetto,* and *Borghese.*

The Phonogram *dge*

The phonogram **dge** comes from Old English and is pronounced with a soft *g* and a short vowel sound. The *d* is inserted before *ge* to keep the vowel short, **preventing it from being pronounced as a long vowel**.

Compare the words **rage** and **badge**:
- In *rage*, the vowel sound is long because it is followed by a single consonant before *e*.
- In *badge*, the *d* prevents the vowel from becoming long, ensuring a short "a" sound instead.

Thus, the *d* in *dge* is a spelling rule that signals a short vowel sound before the soft *g*.

Examples: *Bridge, Drudge, Fidget, Fudge, Judge, Ledge, Lodge, Hedge, Knowledge.*

Activity 46: Fill in the blanks with the most appropriate word from the word bank. Use the sentence context to guide your choices.

Note: This exercise reinforces the usage of words covered in the last two lessons, focusing on the soft and hard "c" and "g" as well as other spelling rules related to these letters. If you're unsure about a word's meaning, look it up in a dictionary and record its definition in the space provided.

Academic	Analog	Crypto	Epilogue	Pathogenic
Accurate	Antagonize	Digest	Fatigue	Reluctant
Aggravate	Autocratic	Disregard	Indigenous	Spaghetti
Agility	Colleague	Egyptian	Judge	Strategic
Allergy	Corporate	Encourage	Knowledge	Toxicology

1. The CEO emphasized the importance of _____________________ responsibility, urging businesses to adopt ethical and sustainable practices.

2. The forensic scientist conducted a _____________________ analysis to determine whether the victim had been exposed to harmful chemicals.

3. Many investors are exploring _____________________ currencies as an alternative to traditional banking systems.

4. The professor received an award for his outstanding contributions to the _____________________ community, particularly in historical research.

Dictionary Work

Academic	Analog	Crypto	Epilogue	Pathogenic
Accurate	Antagonize	Digest	Fatigue	Reluctant
Aggravate	Autocratic	Disregard	Indigenous	Spaghetti
Agility	Colleague	Egyptian	Judge	Strategic
Allergy	Corporate	Encourage	Knowledge	Toxicology

5. Doctors must rely on _____________________ diagnostic tests to determine the best treatment for their patients.

6. Despite the pay increase, he was _____________________ to accept the promotion due to the long working hours.

7. The ruler maintained an _____________________ government, allowing no dissent or opposition from his advisors.

8. The athlete's _____________________ and quick reflexes gave her an advantage in competitive gymnastics.

9. The company's _____________________ planning helped it survive economic downturns and stay ahead of competitors.

10. The human body takes several hours to fully _____________________ a large meal, depending on the type of food consumed.

Dictionary Work

Academic	Analog	Crypto	Epilogue	Pathogenic
Accurate	Antagonize	Digest	Fatigue	Reluctant
Aggravate	Autocratic	Disregard	Indigenous	Spaghetti
Agility	Colleague	Egyptian	Judge	Strategic
Allergy	Corporate	Encourage	Knowledge	Toxicology

11. Good leaders __________________________ their teams by recognizing achievements and fostering a positive work environment.

12. She carries an epinephrine injector in case of a severe __________________________ to peanuts.

13. Ancient __________________________ hieroglyphs provide valuable insights into early civilization and religious beliefs.

14. His rude comments seemed designed to __________________________ his opponent rather than engage in constructive debate.

15. Ignoring early warning signs can __________________________ an existing health condition, making treatment more difficult.

16. The supervisor warned that employees who consistently __________________________ safety regulations would face disciplinary action.

Dictionary Work

Academic	Analog	Crypto	Epilogue	Pathogenic
Accurate	Antagonize	Digest	Fatigue	Reluctant
Aggravate	Autocratic	Disregard	Indigenous	Spaghetti
Agility	Colleague	Egyptian	Judge	Strategic
Allergy	Corporate	Encourage	Knowledge	Toxicology

17. Although digital technology dominates today, some photographers still prefer the warm tones of _____________________ film cameras.

18. The novel's _____________________ provided closure by revealing what happened to the characters years later.

19. My _____________________ and I collaborated on a research paper that was later published in an international journal.

20. After working long shifts in the hospital, the nurses experienced extreme _____________________ and needed rest.

21. The Italian restaurant is famous for its homemade _____________________, prepared using a traditional family recipe.

22. The Supreme Court _____________________ ruled in favor of the plaintiff, citing a violation of constitutional rights.

Dictionary Work

Academic	Analog	Crypto	Epilogue	Pathogenic
Accurate	Antagonize	Digest	Fatigue	Reluctant
Aggravate	Autocratic	Disregard	Indigenous	Spaghetti
Agility	Colleague	Egyptian	Judge	Strategic
Allergy	Corporate	Encourage	Knowledge	Toxicology

23. His extensive ___________________ of medieval history made him a sought-after lecturer at universities worldwide.

24. Scientists have developed a vaccine to combat ___________________ bacteria that cause life-threatening diseases.

25. The exhibit showcased ___________________ artifacts from cultures that have inhabited the region for centuries.

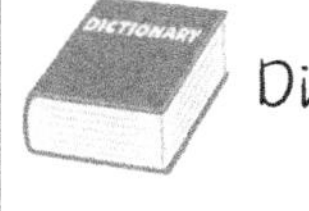

Dictionary Work

Need a break? Head over to the Take a Break page for free fun crossword and word search puzzles created just for you. Scan the QR code or visit the link below to get started!

https://natashascripts.com/takeabreak-spelling-puzzles/

Lesson 25: Adding Suffixes to Words Ending in *ce and ge*

In the previous two lessons, we learned that the silent *e* following *c* or *g* makes them soft. When a root word contains a soft *c* or *g*, such as *peace* or *manage*, adding a suffix must preserve the soft pronunciation. Ensuring the soft sound remains is essential in these cases.

Rule 1
When adding a suffix that begins with *a*, or *o*, to a word ending in *-ce* or *-ge*, the silent *e* is retained to preserve the soft *c* or *g* pronunciation.

Examples:

enforce → enforce**able**
exchange → exchange**able**
advantage → advantage**ous**

Rule 2
When adding a suffix that begins with a consonant to a word ending in *-ce* or *-ge*, the silent *e* is retained to preserve the soft *c* or *g* pronunciation.

Examples:

peace → peace**ful**   announce → announce**ment**
revenge → revenge**ful**   engage → engage**ment**

price → price**less**   strange → strange**ness**
age → age**less**   fierce → fierce**ness**

Note: If the silent "e" is not retained, "c" and "g" would take on a hard pronunciation, as explained in the previous lessons.

<u>Rule 3</u>
When adding a suffix that begins with *e*, or *i*, to a word ending in *-ce* or *-ge*, the silent *e* is dropped because the added vowel suffix already ensures the soft *c* or *g* pronunciation.

Examples:

coerce → coerc**ed**
cringe → cring**ed**

trace → trac**er**
change → chang**er**

practice → practic**ing**
purge → purg**ing**

 **Activity 47: Add the indicated suffix to each base word and write the new word in the blank space, applying the three rules covered in this lesson.**

1. Fringe + -ed = _______________________

2. Camouflage + -able = _______________________

3. Pronounce + -ment = _______________________

4. Voice + -less = _______________________

5. Dance + -er = _______________________

6. Grace + -ful = _______________________

7. Trace + -ing = _______________________

8. Salvage + -able = _______________________

9. Submerge + -ed = _______________________

10. Outrage + -ous = _______________________

11. Enhance + -ment = _______________________

12. Exchange + -able = _______________________

13. Voice + -ing = _______________________

14. Defense + -less = _______________________

15. Juice + -er = _______________________

Lesson 26: Spelling Patterns with *au* and *aw*

The phonograms *au* and *aw* represent the same vowel sound, as heard in author and lawyer, and originate from French and Latin. Their spelling patterns are mutually exclusive, meaning that when one phonogram follows a particular pattern, the other does not. Found in both common and advanced vocabulary, these phonograms generally follow consistent spelling conventions, with only a few exceptions.

The Phonograms *au* and *aw*

The phonogram *au* is commonly found in the following positions:

1. At the beginning of a word
- Examples: auburn, auction, audacity, audible, augment, author, auto.

2. In the first syllable of a word
- Examples: cauliflower (<u>*cau*</u> – *li – flow – er*), causation (<u>*cau*</u> – *sa – tion*), caution (<u>*cau*</u> – *tion*), claustrophobia (<u>*claus*</u> – *tro – pho – bi – a*).

3. In the middle of one-syllable words.
- Examples: cause, fraud, sauce.

4. In the final syllable of a word.
- Examples: applause (*ap* – <u>*plause*</u>), assault (*as* – <u>*sault*</u>), cosmonaut (*cos* – *mo* – <u>*naut*</u>).

Important Note: *Au* is not found at the end of English words. However, some French-derived words end in *-eau*, which retains its original French spelling, such as:
- Examples: bureau, beau, plateau, château.

The phonogram *aw* follows distinct patterns that do not overlap with *au*:

1. At the end of a word, especially single-syllable words.
- Examples: claw, draw, law, saw.

2. At the end of a syllable in a multi-syllabic word.
- Examples: lawyer (*__law__ – yer*), hacksaw (*hack – __saw__*), rickshaw (*rick – __shaw__*), outlaw (*out – __law__*), unlawfulness (*un – __law__ – ful – ness*).

3. Before *n* or *l*.
- Examples: crawl, lawn, prawn.

Note: While the phonogram aw can also produce a different sound, as heard in awake and aware, this lesson focuses on the sound that aw shares with au. The alternative pronunciation of aw does not usually cause confusion in spelling.

Because these patterns are not absolute, and some words do not follow the typical spelling conventions, the best approach is to identify words that you find difficult and practice them regularly until their spelling becomes familiar.

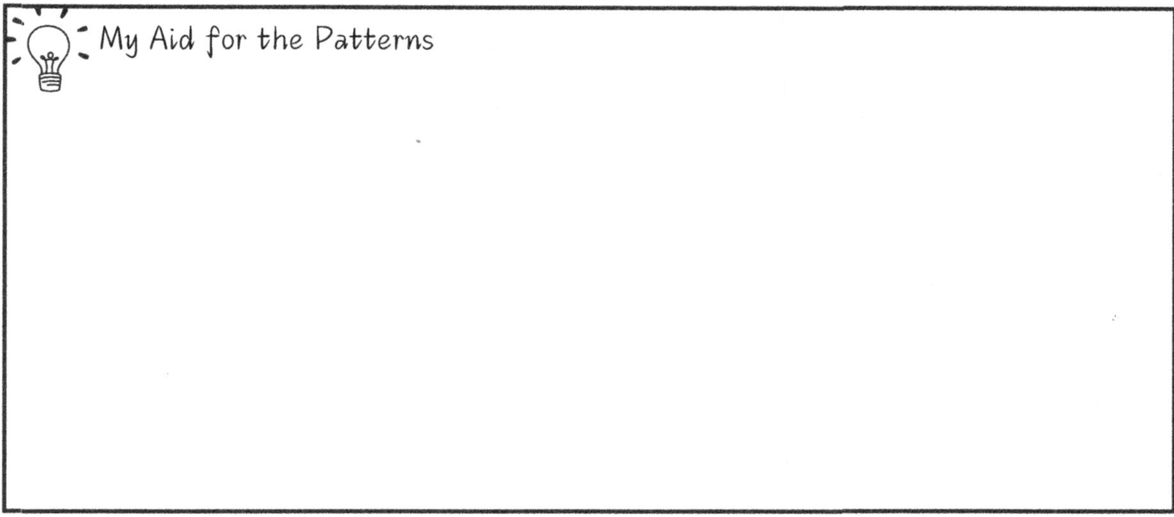

   SPELLING FOR ADULTS © 2025

Activity 48: Complete each sentence with the correct word from the word bank. Pay attention to the context to choose the most appropriate word.

Auction	Authentic	Crawling	Lawyer
Audience	Autograph	Drawback	Outlaw
Audit	Automate	Flawless	Prawn
Augment	Autonomous	Hackshaw	Rawness
Author	Autopilot	Lawful	Withdraw

1. The company hired an external firm to conduct an _____________________ of its financial records after an internal discrepancy was discovered.

2. She decided to _____________________ her skills by taking an advanced certification course in digital marketing.

3. During the police investigation, the suspect's nervous _____________________ was noted as a possible sign of deception.

4. The best-selling _____________________ gave an insightful talk on the process of writing compelling novels.

5. The stolen artwork was recovered and verified as _____________________ by forensic specialists.

6. After months of searching, they finally found a _____________________ house that was legally compliant with zoning laws.

7. He carefully avoided stepping on the baby, who was _____________________ on the floor.

8. The company planned to _____________________ several manual processes to improve efficiency and reduce costs.

9. The famous actor was met by a large _____________________ of fans at the book signing event.

Auction	**Authentic**	**Crawling**	**Lawyer**
Audience	**Autograph**	**Drawback**	**Outlaw**
Audit	**Automate**	**Flawless**	**Prawn**
Augment	**Autonomous**	**Hackshaw**	**Rawness**
Author	**Autopilot**	**Lawful**	**Withdraw**

10. The fugitive was declared an ___________________ by the authorities after evading capture for years.

11. She refused to sign the contract until her ___________________ reviewed every clause carefully.

12. The tech industry is moving toward ___________________ systems, where machines can operate without human intervention.

13. The biggest ___________________ of working remotely is the lack of face-to-face collaboration with colleagues.

14. During the emergency, he had to ___________________ a large sum of money from his savings account.

15. She proudly displayed the framed ___________________ of her favorite musician in her office.

16. The seafood restaurant is known for its fresh ___________________, imported daily from the coast.

17. The athlete's performance was so ___________________ that the judges gave her a perfect score.

18. The ___________________ house sold an original painting for $2 million at last night's auction.

19. The carpenter used a ___________________ to cut through the thick metal pipe.

20. The pilot switched to ___________________ mode once the plane reached cruising altitude.

Lesson 27: Spelling Patterns with *ou* and *ow*

The phonograms *ou* and *ow* share a similar sound, making it difficult to determine which one to use in spelling. However, as with many aspects of English, there are fairly reliable conventions that help guide these choices. These two phonograms are closely related because *w* often replaces *u* in certain positions. This substitution, known as an auxiliary vowel, typically occurs when the next letter is a vowel. Since English rarely allows three consecutive vowels within a word, replacing *u* with *w* helps maintain the flow of pronunciation and spelling. For example, *coward* (which would otherwise be *couard)*, *towel* (*touel*), *vowel* (*vouel*), and *prowess* (*prouess*) follow this pattern.

How do I know when to spell a word with *ou* or *ow*?

---

1. Position of the Word:
- **Beginning or Middle of a Word:** The *ou/ow* sound is typically spelled with *ou* when it appears at the beginning or in the middle of a word.
  - Examples: out, house, found.

- **End of a Word:** When the *ou/ow* sound occurs at the end of a word, it is usually spelled with *ow*.
  - Examples: allow, brow, cow.
    - Note: The phonogram *ow* can also represent a long *o* sound, as in *snow, blow, borrow,* and *shadow*. The convention that *ow* typically appears at the end of a word applies to this pronunciation as well.

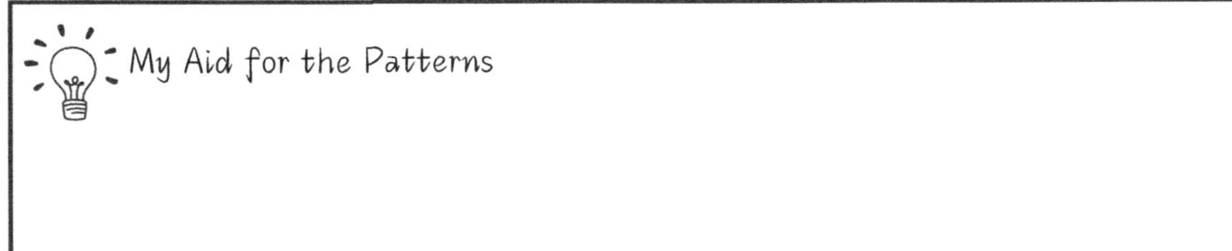

2. Before *n* or *l*:
- The *ou/ow* sound is often spelled with **ow** when it appears before *n* or *l*, typically at the end of a word, but in some cases, it can also occur in the middle of a word.
  - Examples: down, owl, fowl, acknowledge, knowledge.

BUT
- If the *ou/ow* sound is followed by *n or l* plus another consonant, **ou** is generally used.
  - Examples: count, ground, mouth, mountain, counsel.

3. Two-Syllable Words:
- In two-syllable words where the first syllable contains the *ou/ow* sound and is stressed, and the second syllable ends with *er* or *el*, the *ou/ow* sound is often spelled with **ow**.
  - Examples: flower, tower, towel.

Although these patterns are fairly reliable, the best approach is to identify words that you find challenging and practice them regularly.

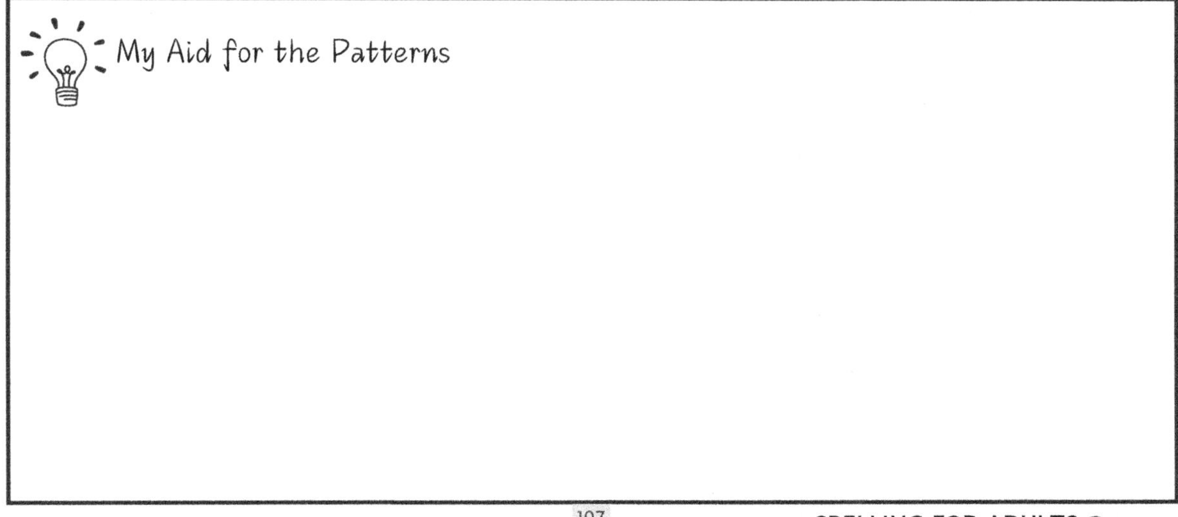

Activity 49: Complete each word by inserting *ou* or *ow*, following the spelling conventions learned in this lesson.

Acc____nt

Am____nt

Anyh____

Ar____nd

Ar____se

Ast____nd

Av____

B____nce

B____nd

B____t

Breakd____n

Br____n

Cl____d

Comp____nd

Conf____nd

C____ch

C____ntd____n

C____nselor

C____nter

Cr____n

Fishb____l

F____nder

G____n

Homegr____n

H____l

J____l

Kn____n

N____

____tgr____n

Overthr____n

R____te

Spr____t

St____t

V____ch

Lesson 28: Spelling Patterns with *ough* and *augh*

The phonograms *ough* and *augh* are among the oldest spellings in English, inherited from Old English and Middle English in the late 14th century. While these phonograms share some sounds, *ough* is the more complex of the two, having the greatest number of pronunciations.

Both *ough* and *augh* appear only at the end of a base word or before a *t*. This rule is useful because it limits where these phonograms can occur, helping spellers eliminate them from words where *au* appears at the beginning, such as *auction* or *author*. However, this rule does not tell us when to use *ough* or *augh* in spelling, as there are no strict conventions governing their placement.

The good news is that words containing *ough* and *augh* are relatively few, making them easier to learn with practice. By familiarizing yourself with their common spellings and pronunciations, you can master them in a short period of time.

The different sounds of *ough*

The phonogram *ough* has at least four different pronunciations. Since there are no rules or conventions that dictate why certain words are spelled with *ough*, studying their sounds becomes even more important. Recognizing these pronunciations helps you gain greater control over your learning journey.

1. The long *o* sound as in *though*.

2. The long *u* sound as in *through*.

3. The *aw* sound as in *thought*.

4. The *ou* sound as in *drought*.

5. The *f* sound as in *cough* and *rough*.

The different sounds of a*ugh*

The phonogram a*ugh* is simpler than *ough* as it has only two sounds:

6. The *aw* sound as in *caught*.

7. The *f* sound as in *laugh*.

While there are several words that follow the first pattern, only a few words follow the second. In fact, laugh, laughed, laughing, and laughter are the only commonly used words where *augh* is pronounced as *f*.

 # Activity 50: Read the rhyming word to ensure correct pronunciation, then say each *ough and augh* word while writing it three times.

The *ough* Phonogram

1. The long *o* sound, rhyming with *go*.

alth**ough** _____________ _____________ _____________

dough _____________ _____________ _____________

though _____________ _____________ _____________

2. The long *u* sound, rhyming with *blue*.

thr**ough** _____________ _____________ _____________

throughout _____________ _____________ _____________

breakthrough _____________ _____________ _____________

3. The *aw* sound, rhyming with *caught*.

th**ough**t _____________ _____________ _____________

bought _____________ _____________ _____________

brought _____________ _____________ _____________

fought _____________ _____________ _____________

ought _____________ _____________ _____________

wrought _____________ _____________ _____________

4. The _ou_ sound, rhyming with _plow_.

dr**ough**t   _________________   _________________

5. The _f_ sound, rhyming with _cuff_.

c**ough**   _________   _________   _________

enough   _________   _________   _________

rough   _________   _________   _________

tough   _________   _________   _________

trough   _________   _________   _________

The _augh_ Phonogram

6. The _aw_ sound, rhyming with _thought_.

c**augh**t   _________   _________   _________

distraught   _________   _________   _________

daughter   _________   _________   _________

fraught   _________   _________   _________

onslaught   _________   _________   _________

naughty   _________   _________   _________

slaughter   _________   _________   _________

taught   _________   _________   _________

7. _Augh_ pronounced as _f_.

laugh   _________   _________   _________

laughed   _________   _________   _________

laughing   _________   _________   _________

laughter   _________   _________   _________

Lesson 29: Spelling Patterns with *ei* and *ie*

Spelling words with *ie* and *ei* can feel unpredictable, but there are practical guidelines that simplify the decision. You may have heard the old rhyme:

> *I* before *e*, except after *c*,
> or when sounding like *a* in *neighbor* and *weigh*,
> or when sounding like *eye* in *seismic* and *height*.

While this rhyme captures some general patterns, English is full of exceptions. Instead of relying on memorization alone, this lesson breaks down the rules logically so you can spell these tricky words with confidence.

Rule 1
- **When a word has a long *ee* sound, as in *believe*, and is NOT followed by the consonant *c*, the order of *i* and *e* is *ie*.**

Rule 2
- **When the long *ee* sound is followed by a *c*, the order changes to *ei*.**

Rule 3
- **When a word has a long *ay* sound, as in *neighbor*, the order of *i* and *e* is *ei*.**

Rule 4
- **When a word has a long *eye* sound, like in *height*, the order is also *ei*.**

Refer to the table below to visualize these rules from the traditional rhyme, and then we will examine the exceptions to these patterns.

SOUND	CONSONANT	ORDER	EXAMPLES	EXCEPTIONS
ee	any	**ie**	**die**sel g**rie**f **chie**f a**chie**ve **yie**ld **sie**ge	patient quotient friend
ee	**c**	**ei**	per**cei**ve **cei**ling de**cei**ve con**cei**ve re**cei**pt de**cei**t	ancient sufficient conscience proficient efficient species
ay	any	**ei**	**nei**ghbor **wei**gh sur**vei**llance **slei**gh **vei**n **wei**ght **rei**ndeer **ei**ght **rei**n	counterfeit sovereign surfeit
eye	any, but usually following "h"	**ei**	apart**hei**d **hei**ght **hei**st Fahren**hei**t	die lie tie pie

Exceptions

Rule 1 states that if a word has a long *ee* vowel sound, the order should be *ie*. However, there are exceptions where a short vowel sound still takes the *ie* order. Let's review the few words that fall into this exception:

patient   quotient   friend

Rule 2 states that when the long *ee* sound is followed by a *c*, the order typically changes to *ei*. However, there are exceptions to this rule:

ancient   proficient   glacier

sufficient   efficient

conscience   omniscient

deficient   species

Rule 3 states that if a word has a long *ay* sound, as in *neighbor*, the order of *i* and *e* is *ei*. However, there are a few words that use the *ei* order without having the *ay* sound, instead having a short *i* sound:

counterfeit   sovereign   surfeit

Rule 4 states that when a word has a long *eye* sound, as in *height*, the order is *ei*. However, there are a few words with the *eye* sound that follow the *ie* order instead.

die lie tie pie

Activity 51: Answer the following questions in complete sentences. Use the bolded word in your response. If you're unsure about the meaning, check a dictionary before writing your answer.

1. What is an **ancient** structure or tradition that still fascinates people today?

2. Have you ever had to **believe** in yourself to overcome a challenge? Describe the situation.

3. What is the most meaningful gift or recognition you have ever **received**?

4. In what situations is it most important to be **patient**, and how do you handle impatience?

____

____

____

5. Have you ever found yourself in a situation where you didn't have **sufficient** time or resources to complete something? How did you manage?

____

____

____

6. Why do you think people try to produce **counterfeit** money or goods? How can consumers protect themselves?

____

____

____

7. What's a task or process in your daily life that you have made more **efficient** over time?

____

____

____

8. What is one personal or professional goal you hope to **achieve** in the next year?

____

____

____

9. How do people cope with grief, and what advice would you give someone experiencing loss?

____

____

____

10. How do first impressions shape the way we **perceive** people, and can those perceptions change over time?

____

____

____

11. Have you ever noticed surveillance being used in a public place or at work? How did it affect your sense of security or privacy?

____

____

____

Note: Since responses will vary based on personal experiences, there are no answers in the answer key for this activity.

    SPELLING FOR ADULTS ©2025

 **Activity 52: Review the list of words below and choose at least five words that you find challenging or need extra practice with. Write each selected word three times in the table provided to reinforce correct spelling.**

<table>
<tr><td colspan="2">ei Words</td><td colspan="2">ie Words</td></tr>
<tr><td>Ceiling</td><td>Receive</td><td>Believe</td><td>Omniscient</td></tr>
<tr><td>Conceive</td><td>Rein</td><td>Chief</td><td>Proficient</td></tr>
<tr><td>Counterfeit</td><td>Sovereign</td><td>Conscience</td><td>Siege</td></tr>
<tr><td>Deceit</td><td>Surveillance</td><td>Deficient</td><td>Species</td></tr>
<tr><td>Deceive</td><td>Vein</td><td>Efficient</td><td>Sufficient</td></tr>
<tr><td>Neighbor</td><td>Weigh</td><td>Glacier</td><td>Yield</td></tr>
<tr><td>Perceive</td><td>Weight</td><td></td><td></td></tr>
</table>

 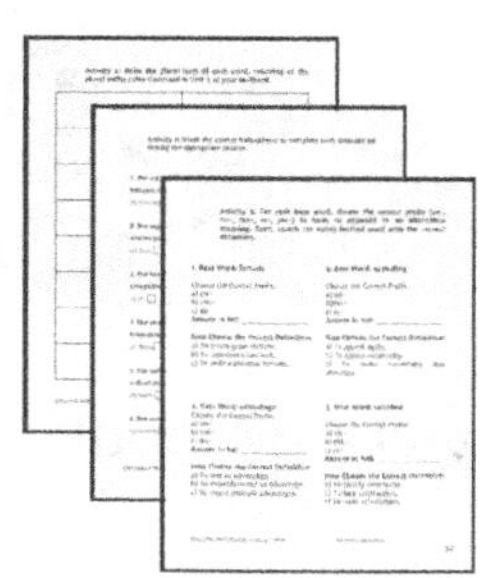

Supplementary Practice Program for Adults

To reinforce what you've learned in this unit, download and print the corresponding worksheets by visiting the following webpage or scanning the QR code.

https://natashascripts.com/spelling-extra-practice-adults/

PROGRESS PORTAL 2: Reflect and Assess

Another milestone reached—great job on completing Module Two!

This module deepened your understanding of spelling patterns, helping you recognize when to use different suffixes, prefixes, and phonograms. You've worked through rules that strengthen your spelling accuracy and make word formation more predictable. Now, let's see how well you've grasped these concepts!

Head to the Progress Portal to:
- Complete your Module 2 test to track your progress.
- Identify which spelling patterns still need extra focus.
- Set a clear plan for Module 3.

Step 1: Take the assessment online by scanning the QR code or visiting https://natashascripts.com/progressportals/

Password for Progress Portal 2, Assessment 2: **ExpandingSkills4-7**

Step 2: Review your results and record your score and test date on the next page.

Step 3: Reflect on your progress and plan your next steps by completing the prompts below.

Assessment 2

Score:

____

Date:

____

Reflection

1. What concepts or skills from Units 4-7 do you feel confident about?

2. Which areas or topics do you find most challenging, and why?

3. What strategy can you use to improve in these areas?
(*E.g., review examples or practice tricky words daily.*)

Goal-Setting

1. Write down one specific goal you want to achieve before completing the next three units. (*E.g., "Master the spelling of homophones by practicing 10 sentences daily."*)

2. What steps will you take to achieve this goal? (*E.g., Use the supplementary practice file, revisit unit examples, or create personal memory aids.*)

3. How will you measure your success? (*E.g., Taking the online test multiple times until I achieve a score above 70%.*)

MODULE 3:

Word Knowledge and Writing Communication

- **Unit 8: Commonly Confused Words and Syllable Practice**
  - Lesson 30: More Commonly Confused Words
  - Lesson 31: Advanced Syllable Practice

- **Unit 9: Word Origins and Root Words**
  - Lesson 32: Greek and Latin Roots
  - Lesson 33: Latin Derived Academic Vocabulary

- **Unit 10: Writing Fundamentals for Everyday and Professional Communication**
  - Lesson 34: Organizing Main Points for Writing
  - Lesson 35: Practical Everyday Writing

- **Progress Portal 3: Reflect and Assess –** *A final checkpoint to evaluate your progress, strengthen areas that need improvement, and prepare for real-world application of spelling and writing skills.*

Unit 8: Commonly Confused Words and Syllable Practice

Introduction
This unit builds on Unit 1 by focusing on intermediate and advanced commonly confused words while also practicing the syllabification of challenging multi-syllabic vocabulary.

Unit Overview
In the lessons of this unit you will explore pairs of similar-sounding words presented in visual boxes that include:
- Clear definitions
- Model sentences
- Explanations of key differences
- Space to create your own mnemonic aids

Additionally, you will practice breaking down complex words into syllables—a critical skill for accurately spelling vocabulary used in both academic and professional settings. Through these exercises, you will refine your ability to distinguish between easily confused words and develop effective strategies for handling advanced vocabulary.

By the end of this unit, you will be able to:
- **Accurately syllabify multi-syllabic words to improve your spelling precision.**
- **Spell and effectively apply essential vocabulary for academic and professional use.**

Recognizing that these activities can be demanding, you are encouraged to take short breaks as needed to refresh your focus and maximize your learning experience.

Supplementary Practice Program
To further reinforce the lessons in this unit, you can download the corresponding supplementary worksheets designed for extra practice. The link and QR code to access these worksheets are provided at the end of this unit.

In Module 1, we covered basic homophones—words that sound the same but have different spellings and meanings—such as *there*, *their*, and *they're*. These words are frequently used in both spoken and written communication, making it essential to know their correct usage.

In this lesson, we will continue working with commonly confused homophones, but at a more intermediate level. Some of these words, like *affect* and *effect*, are often misused because their meanings are closely related, while others, like *waive* and *wave*, are spelled differently despite sounding the same.

Each word in this lesson will be presented with its definition, and you will have space to create your own mnemonic or memory aid to reinforce correct spelling and meaning. In the practice activities, you will apply these words in varied exercises, ensuring that spelling practice is reinforced through real-world usage.

Words Practiced in this Lesson
Affect, Effect, Advice, Advise, Accept, Except, Complement, Compliment, Desert, Dessert, Capital, Capitol, Loose, Lose, Principal, Principle, Stationary, Stationery, Waive, Wave.

 SPELLING FOR ADULTS ©2025

Affect

The new policy will **<u>affect</u>** how employees are scheduled.

Affect (verb) – To influence or change something.

Effect

The change in management had a positive **<u>effect</u>** on workplace morale.

Effect (noun) – A result or outcome of an action.

Key Difference: *Affect* is an action (verb) that influences something, while *effect* is the result (noun) of that action.

 **My Memory Aid**

Advice

She gave me great **<u>advice</u>** on starting a business.

Advice (noun) – A recommendation or suggestion.

Advise

I would **<u>advise</u>** you to review the contract carefully.

Advise (verb) – To give guidance or a suggestion.

Key Difference: *Advice* is a thing (noun) that you give, while *advise* is the action (verb) of giving it.

 **My Memory Aid**

Accept

She **accepted** the job offer without hesitation.

Accept (verb) – To receive or agree to something.

Except

Everyone was invited to the meeting **except** John.

Except – To exclude something or make an exception. (preposition/conjunction/verb)

Key Difference: *Accept* means to receive or agree, while *except* indicates exclusion or an exception.

 **My Memory Aid**

Complement

The blue tie perfectly **complements** his suit.

Complement (noun/verb) – Something that completes or enhances another thing.

Compliment

She gave him a **compliment** on his presentation skills.

Compliment (noun/verb) – A polite expression of praise or admiration.

Key Difference: *Complement* means to enhance or complete, while *compliment* means to give praise.

 **My Memory Aid**

Desert   Dessert

The Sahara is the largest **desert** in the world.

**Desert (noun) – A dry, barren land with little rainfall.
(also a verb meaning** *to abandon*)

She ordered chocolate cake for **dessert** after dinner.

Dessert (noun) – A sweet dish served at the end of a meal.

Key Difference: A *desert* is a hot, dry place, while *dessert* is a sweet treat after a meal.

My Memory Aid

Capital   Capitol

Investors need a lot of **capital** to start a business.

Capital (noun) – Refers to wealth, a city that serves as the seat of government, or uppercase letters.

The lawmakers met inside the **Capitol** to debate the new bill.

Capitol (noun) – A government building where a legislative body meets.

Key Difference: *Capital* relates to money, a main city, or uppercase letters, while *capitol* only refers to a government building.

My Memory Aid

Loose

My shoelaces are <u>**loose**</u>, so I need to tie them again.

**Loose (adjective) – Not tight or securely fixed.
(also a verb meaning *to set free*)**

Lose

If you don't keep track of your keys, you might <u>**lose**</u> them again.

Lose (verb) – To misplace something or be deprived of it.

Key Difference: *Loose* describes something not tight or secure, while *lose* means to misplace or fail to keep something.

 **My Memory Aid**

Principal

The school <u>**principal**</u> addressed the students during assembly.

Principal (noun/adjective) – The head of a school (noun) or the most important part of something (adjective).

Principle

He refused to lie because of his strong <u>**principles**</u>.

Principle (noun) – A fundamental belief, rule, or truth.

Key Difference: A *principal* can be a school leader or the main part of something while *principle* is a moral rule or belief.

 **My Memory Aid**

Stationary

The train remained **stationary** for several minutes before departing.

Stationary (adjective) – Not moving or fixed in place.

Stationery

She bought new **stationery** for her office, including notebooks and pens.

Stationery (noun) – Writing materials such as paper, envelopes, and pens.

Key Difference: *Stationary* means still or unmoving, while *stationery* refers to writing supplies.

 **My Memory Aid**

Waive

The bank agreed to **waive** the late fee as a courtesy.

Waive (verb) – To give up a right, claim, or requirement voluntarily.

Wave

She gave a friendly **wave** as she left the office.

Wave (noun/verb) – A movement of the hand as a signal or a movement in water.

Key Difference: *Waive* means to forgo or give up something, while *wave* refers to a motion, either in water or with the hand.

 **My Memory Aid**

Activity 53: Read the definition carefully and select the correct word from the given pair.

1. Which word means "to misplace something or fail to keep it"?
a) Loose
b) Lose

2. Which word means "not moving or fixed in place"?
a) Stationary
b) Stationery

3. Which word means "something that enhances or completes another thing"?
a) Complement
b) Compliment

4. Which word means "a movement of the hand as a signal or a movement in water"?
a) Waive
b) Wave

5. Which word means "the head of a school or the most important part of something"?
a) Principal
b) Principle

6. Which word means "wealth, an important city, or uppercase letters"?
a) Capital
b) Capitol

7. Which word means "a fundamental belief, rule, or truth"?
a) Principal
b) Principle

8. Which word means "to give up a right, claim, or requirement voluntarily"?
a) Waive
b) Wave

9. Which word means "not tight or securely fixed"?
a) Loose
b) Lose

10. Which word means "a polite expression of praise or admiration"?
a) Complement
b) Compliment

11. Which word means "a building where a legislative body meets"?
a) Capital
b) Capitol

12. Which word means "writing materials such as paper, envelopes, and pens"?
a) Stationary
b) Stationery

13. Which word means "a sweet dish served at the end of a meal"?
a) Desert
b) Dessert

14. Which word means "to influence or change something"?
a) Affect
b) Effect

15. Which word means "to exclude something or make an exception"?
a) Accept
b) Except

16. Which word means "a dry, barren land with little to no rainfall"?
a) Desert
b) Dessert

17. Which word means "a recommendation or suggestion given to someone"?
a) Advice
b) Advise

18. Which word means "to willingly receive or agree to something"?
a) Accept
b) Except

19. Which word means "to give guidance or suggest something"?
a) Advice
b) Advise

20. Which word means "a result or outcome of an action"?
a) Affect
b) Effect

Activity 54: Identify the correct word based on the context of the sentence.

Advice / Advise
1. The financial consultant will _______________ you on the best investment options for retirement.
2. The lawyer gave his client important _______________ on how to proceed with the case.

Affect / Effect
3. The policy change had a positive _______________ on workplace efficiency, reducing unnecessary meetings.
4. The new manager's leadership style began to _______________ the team's morale, making them more motivated.

Accept / Except

5. He had to _______________ the job offer quickly before they chose another candidate.

6. Everyone was excited about the company retreat _______________ for Jim, who preferred working from home.

Complement / Compliment

7. Her skills in writing _______________ his expertise in graphic design, making them a strong creative team.

8. She blushed when her coworker gave her a _______________ on her presentation skills.

Desert / Dessert

9. After dinner, she treated herself to a rich chocolate _______________ that perfectly ended the meal.

10. The explorers stocked up on supplies before crossing the harsh _______________, where water was scarce.

Capital / Capitol

11.Security was increased around the _______________ before the important legislative meeting.

12. Many entrepreneurs struggle to raise enough _______________ to start their businesses.

Loose / Lose

13. The screws on the chair were _______________, making it wobbly and unstable.

14. He didn't want to _______________ his keys again, so he placed them in the same spot every day.

Principal / Principle

15. She refused to take the shortcut because it went against her _______________ of fairness and honesty.

16. The _______________ of the high school announced new policies to improve student discipline.

Stationary / Stationery

17. The train remained _______________ at the platform while passengers boarded.

18. She bought elegant _______________ for writing thank-you notes.

Waive / Wave

19. She gave a small _______________ to her friend across the street before heading into the café.

20. The university decided to _______________ the application fee for students facing financial hardship.

Activity 55: Decide if the bolded word in each sentence is correctly used according to the context of the sentence.

1. She was happy to **except** the invitation to the event.

2. The new law had a significant **effect** on local businesses.

3. She gave a quick **wave** before boarding the train.

4. Everyone attended the meeting **except** Mark, who was out sick.

5. He ordered chocolate cake for **desert** after dinner.

6. The company decided to **wave** the application fee for new customers.

7. The bad weather will **effect** our travel plans.

8. The explorers traveled across the scorching **desert** for days.

9. If you don't double-check your answers, you might **lose** valuable points on the test.

10. He turned down the shady business deal because it went against his **principals**.

Mastering the spelling of multi-syllabic words is essential for professional writing and workplace communication. In Unit 1, you practiced syllabification, a powerful strategy for improving spelling accuracy. This technique becomes even more effective with longer words containing two, three, or even four syllables.

In this lesson, you will focus on spelling important words that are commonly used in professional and academic settings—words that many people find challenging to spell accurately. These words often contain tricky letter combinations, irregular sounds, or silent letters, making them harder to retain.

By breaking a word into its natural rhythmic syllables, you can focus on one part at a time, increasing your chances of spelling it correctly. As you work through this lesson, take the time to look up and write down any unfamiliar words.

Practiced in this Lesson:

Argument	Completely	Government	Persistent	Vacuum
Basically	Consensus	Harass	Plagiarism	Vicious
Beginning	Curiosity	Liaison	Privilege	Zucchini
Broccoli	Disappear	License	Questionnaire	
Business	Disappoint	Maintenance	Succinct	
Calendar	Entrepreneur	Occasion	Supersede	
Category	Environment	Occurrence	Tomorrow	
Committee	Fluorescent	Parallel	Unforeseen	

     SPELLING FOR ADULTS ©2025

Activity 56: Break each target word into syllables, using hyphens (-) to separate them. Then, write the word in its complete form.

Target Word	Syllables	Write in Syllables	Write in Full
Argument	Ar-gu-ment	_____________	_____________
Basically	Ba-si-cal-ly	_____________	_____________
Beginning	Be-gin-ning	_____________	_____________
Broccoli	Broc-co-li	_____________	_____________
Business	Busi-ness	_____________	_____________
Calendar	Cal-en-dar	_____________	_____________
Category	Cat-e-go-ry	_____________	_____________
Committee	Com-mit-tee	_____________	_____________
Completely	Com-plete-ly	_____________	_____________
Consensus	Con-sen-sus	_____________	_____________
Curiosity	Cu-ri-os-i-ty	_____________	_____________
Disappear	Dis-ap-pear	_____________	_____________
Disappoint	Dis-ap-point	_____________	_____________
Entrepreneur	En-tre-pre-neur	_____________	_____________
Environment	En-vi-ron-ment	_____________	_____________
Fluorescent	Fluo-res-cent	_____________	_____________

Target Word	Syllables	Write in Syllables	Write in Full
Government	Gov-ern-ment	_____________	_____________
Harass	Ha-rass	_____________	_____________
Liaison	Li-ai-son	_____________	_____________
License	Li-cense	_____________	_____________
Maintenance	Main-te-nance	_____________	_____________
Occasion	Oc-ca-sion	_____________	_____________
Occurrence	Oc-cur-rence	_____________	_____________
Parallel	Par-al-lel	_____________	_____________
Persistent	Per-sist-ent	_____________	_____________
Plagiarism	Pla-gia-rism	_____________	_____________
Privilege	Priv-i-lege	_____________	_____________
Questionnaire	Ques-tion-naire	_____________	_____________
Succinct	Suc-cinct	_____________	_____________
Supersede	Su-per-sede	_____________	_____________
Tomorrow	To-mor-row	_____________	_____________
Unforeseen	Un-fore-seen	_____________	_____________
Vacuum	Vac-u-um	_____________	_____________
Vicious	Vi-cious	_____________	_____________
Zucchini	Zuc-chi-ni	_____________	_____________

 **Activity 57: In the passage below, some of the bolded words from this lesson have been misspelled. Carefully proofread the passage, identify the words that are spelled incorrectly, and write their correct spelling in the space provided.**

The Entrepreneur's Challenge

The meeting room was illuminated by **fluorescent** lights, casting a stark glow over the long table where the **committee** had gathered. The **entrepreneur**, a young and ambitious woman, had presented her business plan with enthusiasm, only to find herself caught in an unexpected **arguement**. There was no clear **consensus** among the members regarding her proposal, and she could sense their **curiousity** about her ability to handle an unforeseen crisis.

"Expanding into this market would **completely** change our business model," one of the members stated, scanning a **questionnaire** that had been distributed earlier. "But have you considered the legal aspects? You'll need a special **license**, and the **goverment** regulations in this **category** are strict."

She nodded, staying **persistant** despite the skepticism. "I've spoken with a **liaison** from the regulatory office, and they've assured me that compliance is manageable with the right maintenance plan. I understand that this is a major **occurence** in our company's development, but I believe it will **supersede** any short-term challenges."

Despite her confidence, she couldn't shake the feeling that she might **disappoint** some of the more cautious stakeholders. Still, she knew that in the world of business, resilience was a **privilege**, not a guarantee.

Correct Spelling

 **Activity 58: Choose the correct word from the list and rewrite each sentence using it. Replace the bolded word(s) and adjust the sentence as needed while keeping the original meaning.**

Consensus Disappointment Environment Fluorescent Government

License Maintenance Persistent Privilege Unforeseen

1. **Regular upkeep** of machinery is essential for preventing breakdowns.

____

____

2. The **bright** lights in the office made it easier to read at night.

____

____

3. Having access to higher education is **something not everyone gets**.

____

____

4. Many companies are now focusing on creating a sustainable **workplace** for their employees.

____

____

5.The sudden storm caused **unexpected** delays in transportation.

____

____

6. Even after several failures, he **continued trying** to complete the project.

____

____

7. The **state** is responsible for making laws that protect citizens.

____

____

8. She felt **let down** when she didn't win the competition.

____

____

9. Everyone in the team reached a **general agreement** before making the final decision.

____

____

10. Drivers must obtain **official permission** before operating a vehicle on public roads.

____

____

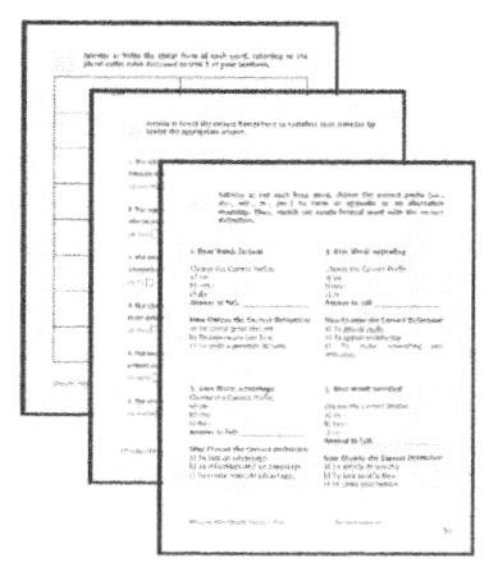

<u>Supplementary Practice Program for Adults</u>

To reinforce what you've learned in this unit, download and print the corresponding worksheets by visiting the following webpage or scanning the QR code.

https://natashascripts.com/spelling-extra-practice-adults/

SPELLING FOR ADULTS ©2025

Unit 9: Understanding Word Origins

Introduction

The English language is a fascinating mosaic. Although its foundation is Germanic, it has absorbed a vast vocabulary from Latin and Greek over the centuries. When the Romans invaded Britain and later when the Norman Conquest introduced French—a Latin-based language—thousands of Latin words entered English. During the Renaissance, scholars further enriched the language by borrowing extensively from Greek, particularly in science, medicine, and academia. In this unit, we delve into Greek and Latin roots to reveal the origins of many words. Studying these roots helps you decipher unfamiliar words by providing clues to their meanings and spellings.

Unit Overview

This unit has two lessons. The first lesson introduces you to basic Greek and Latin roots—such as *bio*, *script*, and others—which form the building blocks of many English words. The second lesson focuses on Latin-derived academic vocabulary—advanced words like *accessible*, *adduce*, *brevity*, and others that are essential in professional and academic contexts. The vocabulary is presented in tables that include each word's origin, definition, and a sample sentence. You will also practice syllabifying, spelling, and using these words in your own sentences.

By the end of this unit, you will be able to:
- Identify common Greek and Latin roots that form the basis of advanced vocabulary.
- Decipher unfamiliar words by recognizing these roots and understanding their meanings.
- Accurately spell and effectively use vocabulary derived from these roots in academic and professional contexts.

Supplementary Practice Program

To further reinforce the lessons in this unit, you can download the corresponding supplementary worksheets designed for extra practice. The link and QR code to access these worksheets are provided at the end of this unit.

Lesson 32: Greek and Latin Roots

This lesson aims to introduce commonly used Greek and Latin roots, strengthen the ability to decipher word meanings by recognizing root connections and reinforce accurate spelling of words derived from these roots.

Understanding basic Greek and Latin roots, such as *audi* (to hear) and *dict* (to say), helps reveal how these roots connect to their English derivatives. Recognizing these foundational elements enables you to decode unfamiliar words and improve spelling accuracy.

Review the following table and identify any Greek or Latin roots that are unfamiliar to you. Use the provided column to mark a ✓ for roots you already know and an ✗ for those you need to practice. You will apply spelling and usage of words formed from these roots in later exercises.

Practiced in This Lesson:

<u>Greek and Latin Roots</u>

Audi	Geo	Micro	Scrib, script
Astro	Graph	Mit, miss	Spec, spect
Bio	Hydr	Path	Struct
Chrono	Junct	Phon	Tele
Dict	Jur	Photo	Therm
Fid	Log, logue	Port	Vis, vid
			Voc

Root	Origin	Definition	Examples	Know this? ✓ ✗
Audi	*Latin*	**Hear, listen, sound**	Audible Auditorium	
Astro	*Greek*	**Star**	Astronomy Astronaut	
Bio	*Greek*	**Life**	Biography Biology	
Chrono	*Greek*	**Time**	Chronological Synchronize	
Dict	*Latin*	**Speak, say**	Dictation Predict	
Fid	*Latin*	**Trust**	Fidelity Confide	
Geo	*Greek*	**Earth**	Geography Geothermal	
Graph	*Greek*	**Write**	Autograph Graphic	
Hydr	*Greek*	**Water**	Hydrant Dehydrated	
Junct	*Latin*	**Join**	Junction Adjunct	
Jur	*Latin*	**Law, right**	Jurisdiction Perjury	
Log, logue	*Greek*	**Word, reason**	Logical Dialogue	

Root	Origin	Definition	Examples	Know this? ✓ ✗
Micro	Greek	Small	Microscope Microbe	
Mit, miss		Send	Submit Emission	
Path	Greek	Feeling, disease	Pathology Empathy	
Phon	Greek	Sound	Microphone Symphony	
Photo	Greek	Light	Photograph Photosynthesis	
Port	Latin	Carry	Portable Transport	
Scrib, script	Latin	Write	Manuscript Describe	
Spec, spect	Latin	Look, see	Spectacle Perspective	
Struct	Latin	Build	Construct Instruct	
Tele	Greek	Far	Television Telepathy	
Therm	Greek	Heat	Thermometer Thermostat	
Vis, vid	Latin	See	Visible Video	
Voc	Latin	Voice, Call	Vocal	

Activity 59: Each word in Column A contains a Greek or Latin root that contributes to its meaning. Match each word to its correct definition in Column B.

Column A

Column B

1. **Hydrothermal**

2. **Destruction**

3. **Inscription**

4. **Exportation**

5. **Cacophony**

6. **Sociopath**

7. **Monologue**

8. **Carbohydrate**

9. **Bibliography**

10. **Indictment**

11. **Anachronism**

12. **Bioidentical**

13. **Auditor**

A) Something that is out of place in time, such as a modern object appearing in a historical setting.

B) A list of books, articles, or other sources used in research or referenced in a document.

C) A person who officially examines financial records for accuracy and compliance.

D) A formal charge or accusation of a serious crime.

E) A substance that closely matches naturally occurring biological compounds in the body.

F) Relating to heated water, especially in geological processes.

G) A speech or performance given by one person, often in a play or presentation.

H) A type of nutrient composed of sugars and starches that provide energy.

I) A person who exhibits antisocial behavior, lacking empathy or remorse.

J) A harsh, jarring mixture of sounds.

K) The act of sending goods or services to another country for trade or sale.

L) A written or engraved marking, often on a monument or document.

M) The process of causing something to be ruined or completely torn down.

1. _____, 2. _____, 3. _____, 4. _____, 5. _____, 6. _____, 7. _____, 8. _____,
9. _____, 10. _____, 11. _____, 12. _____, 13. _____.

 **Activity 60: Now that you have correctly matched each word to its definition, write a clear and accurate sentence using each word. Make sure your sentence demonstrates the word's meaning in context.**

1. Hydrothermal

Example: The island is home to several hydrothermal vents, where seawater is heated by volcanic activity beneath the ocean floor.

2. Destruction

3. Inscription

4. Exportation

5. Cacophony

6. Sociopath

     SPELLING FOR ADULTS ©2025

7. Monologue

____

____

____

8. Carbohydrate

____

____

____

9. Bibliography

____

____

____

10. Indictment

____

____

____

11. Anachronism

____

____

____

12. Bioidentical

____

____

____

13. Auditor

____

____

____

Lesson 33: Latin-Derived Academic Vocabulary

The aim of this lesson is to practice the spelling and usage of professional and academic vocabulary derived from Latin. Many words used in these settings originate from this classical language.

The vocabulary has been carefully selected for its relevance in the workplace and advanced communication. The activities in this lesson are designed to deepen your understanding of each word by referencing its Latin origin. You will first practice writing these words in syllables, then spell them in full, and finally, compose complete sentences using a selection of words from the list. These exercises will help you strengthen your spelling accuracy while applying word meaning in context through structured sentence writing.

Practiced in This Lesson

<u>Latin-Derived Vocabulary</u>

Accessible	Gratuitous	Proponent
Adduce	Impetus	Rationale
Brevity	Increment	Recapitulate
Compulsory	Insolvent	Retrospect
Dispel	Mediate	Seminal
Dividend	Obfuscate	Subsidiary
Exacerbate	Palpable	Transgress
Expediency	Pecuniary	Ubiquitous
Finite	Peremptory	Unequivocal
Fortuitous	Premise	Verbose

Activity 61: This exercise reinforces academic and professional vocabulary through spelling and syllabification. After reading each word's meaning, origin, and example sentence, spell it twice in syllabified form.

Root (Origin)	Word	Meaning	Example Sentence
ced-/cess- (Latin: go, yield)	**Accessible**	Able to be reached or entered	This building is fully **accessible** to people with disabilities.

Ac-ces-si-ble _______________________ _______________________

Root (Origin)	Word	Meaning	Example Sentence
duc-/duct- (Latin: lead, bring forth)	**Adduce**	To offer evidence or proof in support of an argument	The lawyer tried to **adduce** evidence to support his client's claim.

Ad-duce _______________________ _______________________

Root (Origin)	Word	Meaning	Example Sentence
acerb- (Latin: bitter, harsh, sour, sharp)	**Exacerbate**	To make a situation worse	The delay in shipping **exacerbated** customer frustration.

Ex-ac-er-bate _______________________ _______________________

Root (Origin)	Word	Meaning	Example Sentence
ped- (Latin: foot, travel)	**Expediency**	Acting out of convenience rather than principle	The decision was made based on **expediency**, not ethics.

Ex-pe-di-en-cy _______________________ _______________________

Root (Origin)	Word	Meaning	Example Sentence
fin- (Latin: end, limit)	**Finite**	Having limits or measurable boundaries	Natural resources are **finite** and must be used wisely.
Fi - nite _______________		_______________	
fort- (Latin: luck, strength)	**Fortuitous**	Happening by chance rather than by intention	It was purely **fortuitous** that we met at the same café.
For-tu-i-tous _______________		_______________	
pecun- (Latin: money)	**Pecuniary**	Related to money or financial matters	He took the job for **pecuniary** reasons, not passion.
Pe-cu-ni-ar-y _______________		_______________	
per- (Latin: thorough, through) *em-/empt-* (Latin: take, buy)	**Peremptory**	Insisting on immediate attention, not open to challenge	The judge issued a **peremptory** order that could not be appealed.
Per-emp-to-ry _______________		_______________	
pre- (Latin: before)	**Premise**	A statement or assumption forming the basis for reasoning	His argument was built on a flawed **premise**.
Prem-ise _______________		_______________	

Root (Origin)	Word	Meaning	Example Sentence
brev- (Latin: short)	**Brevity**	Conciseness or shortness in speech or writing	The professor appreciated the **brevity** of the report.
Brev-i-ty ________________ ________________			
grat- (Latin: pleasing, free)	**Gratuitous**	Given freely or without cause	The hotel's **gratuitous** refreshments were a relief to the overheated guests.
Gra-tu-i-tous ________________ ________________			
im- (Latin: in, on) *pet-* (Latin: seek, attack, strive towards)	**Impetus**	A force that drives action or movement	The new policy provided **impetus** for economic growth.
Im-pe-tus ________________ ________________			
cre- (Latin: grow, increase)	**Increment**	A small increase or addition over time	Employees received a salary **increment** every year.
In-cre-ment ________________ ________________			
pro- (Latin: forward) *pon-* (Latin: place, put)	**Proponent**	A person who supports or advocates for something	She is a strong **proponent** of renewable energy.
Pro-po-nent ________________ ________________			

Root (Origin)	Word	Meaning	Example Sentence
ratio- (Latin: reason, calculation)	**Rationale**	A logical explanation or justification	The manager explained the **rationale** behind the new policy.
Ra-tion-ale ________________ ________________			
capit- (Latin: head, summary)	**Recapitulate**	To summarize the main points	At the end of the meeting, she **recapitulated** the key takeaways.
Re-ca-pit-u-late ________________ ________________			
pel- (Latin: drive, push)	**Compulsory**	Required by law or rule	Education is **compulsory** for children in most countries.
Com-pul-so-ry ________________ ________________			
in- (Latin: not) *solv-* (Latin: loosen, release)	**Insolvent**	Unable to pay debts	The company became **insolvent** and had to file for bankruptcy.
In-sol-vent ________________ ________________			
retro- (Latin – backward, behind) *spect-* (Latin: look, see)	**Retrospect**	Looking back on past events	In **retrospect**, we should have handled the situation differently.
Ret-ro-spect ________________ ________________			

Root (Origin)	Word	Meaning	Example Sentence
sem- (Latin: seed, scatter)	**Seminal**	Highly influential in a particular field	The researcher published a **seminal** paper on artificial intelligence.
Sem-i-nal ___________________ ___________________			
medi- (Latin: middle, intervene)	**Mediate**	To intervene in a dispute to resolve it	The HR manager had to **mediate** the conflict between employees.
Me-di-ate ___________________ ___________________			
sub- (Latin: under, supporting)	**Subsidiary**	A company controlled by a larger corporation	The tech giant acquired a new **subsidiary** to expand its reach.
Sub-sid-i-ar-y ___________________ ___________________			
trans- (Latin: across, beyond)	**Transgress**	To violate a law, rule, or boundary	Employees who **transgress** company policies may face termination.
Trans-gress ___________________ ___________________			
pell- (Latin: drive, push away)	**Dispel**	To drive away doubts or fears	The report helped **dispel** rumors about the company's future.
Dis-pel ___________________ ___________________			

Root (Origin)	Word	Meaning	Example Sentence
divide- (Latin: separate, share)	**Dividend**	A sum of money paid to shareholders from company profits	Investors were pleased with the high **dividend** payout.
Div-i-dend ___________________ ___________________			
equ- (Latin: equal, balanced, even)	**Unequivocal**	Leaving no doubt; clear and direct	The scientist's findings were **unequivocal** and well-supported.
Un-e-quiv-o-cal ___________________ ___________________			
fusc- (Latin: dark, obscure)	**Obfuscate**	To make something unclear or confusing	The politician's vague answers only **obfuscated** the issue.
Ob-fus-cate ___________________ ___________________			
palpare (Latin: touch or caress)	**Palpable**	Able to be touched, felt, or easily perceived	There was a **palpable** sense of excitement in the crowd.
Pal-pa-ble ___________________ ___________________			
ubi- (Latin: where, position)	**Ubiquitous**	Present everywhere at the same time	Smartphones have become **ubiquitous** in modern life.
U-biq-ui-tous ___________________ ___________________			
verb- (Latin: word)	**Verbose**	Using more words than necessary	His writing style is too **verbose** for an academic paper.
Ver-bose ___________________ ___________________			

 **Activity 62: From the previous activity, select at least eight words you want to practice further, focusing on both spelling and usage. Write each word three times and use it in a sentence, following the example provided.**

Accessible	Accessible	Accessible
The library's online resources are easily accessible to all students, allowing them to study anytime, anywhere.		

SPELLING FOR ADULTS ©2025

 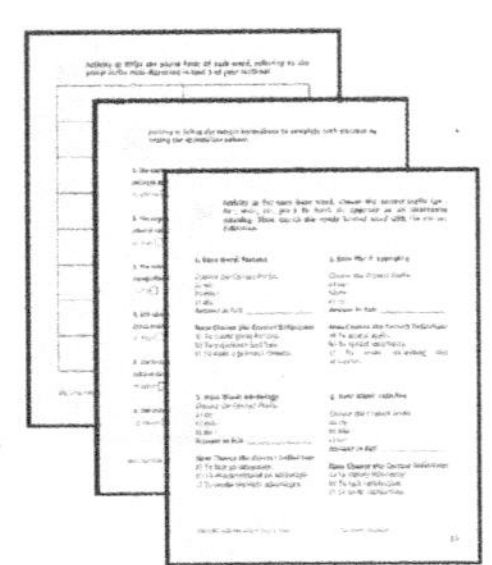

<u>Supplementary Practice Program for Adults</u>

To reinforce what you've learned in this unit, download and print the corresponding worksheets by visiting the following webpage or scanning the QR code.

https://natashascripts.com/spelling-extra-practice-adults/

Unit 10: Writing Fundamentals for Everyday and Professional Communication

Introduction

Have you ever started writing something—an email, a job application, or even a message—only to realize your thoughts feel scattered, repetitive, or unclear? You may have a lot to say, but if your ideas aren't well-organized, your message can become confusing or ineffective.

Unit Overview

This final unit focuses specifically on organizational skills in writing, helping you structure your thoughts and communicate clearly in various contexts. You will learn how to organize your main points using a systematic, step-by-step approach and apply these techniques to real-world tasks. The lessons include practical exercises for composing emails, workplace reports, letters to institutions, complaint letters, and reflective writing for personal growth, all supported by visual aids, tables, and model templates.

By the end of this unit you will be able to:
- Gather your ideas before you start writing.
- Structure your writing in a clear and logical manner.
- Avoid repetition and unnecessary words to keep your message concise.
- Use simple techniques to improve clarity

Supplementary Practice Program

To further reinforce the lessons in this unit, you can download the corresponding supplementary worksheets designed for extra practice. The link and QR code to access these worksheets are provided at the end of this unit.

Lesson 34: Organizing Main Points for Writing

This lesson provides a step-by-step guide on how to gather ideas, organize them coherently, and avoid repetition when writing a formal email. The focus is on professional communication, such as work-related emails or messages for formal settings. While informal emails to family and friends do not strictly require this structure, presenting ideas clearly and concisely is always beneficial.

Thinking through your ideas before writing helps prevent confusion, repetition, and unnecessary details. A well-structured message is easier to understand and more effective in both professional and everyday communication. Therefore, defining the purpose of your communication is essential.

Step 1: Define your Purpose

Before writing, ask yourself:
1. What is my main message?
2. Who is my audience?
3. What key points must I include?

- **Example:** If you're writing an email to request time off, <u>your main message is asking for leave</u>, <u>your audience is your manager</u>, and <u>your key points include your dates and reason</u>.

Step 2: Organize your Ideas using a Simple Structure

Most clear writing follows this order:
1. **Introduction** – A short opening that explains what you're writing about.
2. **Main Points** – Two to three key points, each in its own sentence or paragraph.
3. **Conclusion/Action** – A final sentence to wrap up or request action.

◦ **Example of a Clear and Concise Email Request:**

Subject: Request for Leave – March 10-12

Body:

Dear [Manager's Name],

I hope this email finds you well. I am writing to request leave from March 10 to 12 due to a personal commitment. I will ensure that all my work is up to date before then. Please let me know if you need further details.

Best regards,
[Your Name]

Why this Works:
- No repetition
- Clear key points (date, reason, assurance of work)
- Concise and polite language

Note on Addressing: In many workplaces (U.S.) it is common to address managers by their first name, especially in casual environments like retail or supermarkets. However, in more formal settings, using Mr./Ms. [Last Name] may be more appropriate unless the manager has indicated otherwise. If unsure, start with a formal address.

Organizing Longer Texts

For more detailed writing—such as a report, presentation, or proposal—organizing your thoughts before writing ensures that your message is clear and logical. Two effective methods to do this are:

1. **Bullet Points:** Write down key ideas in short points before turning them into full sentences.
2. **Mind Mapping:** Start with your main idea in the center and branch out key points. and supporting details. This method visually organizes your ideas, making it easier to see connections between points and avoid redundancy.

- ○ **Example Using Bullet Points to Draft a Job Application Cover Letter**

Main Idea	• Why I'm a good fit
Key Point 1	• Relevant experience
Key Point 2	• Key skills that match the job
Key Point 3	• Enthusiasm for the company

- ○ **Example Using a Mind Map for a Workplace Report**

A workplace report often requires structured information and clear communication. Below is an example of how a mind map can help organize ideas for a workplace incident report before writing.

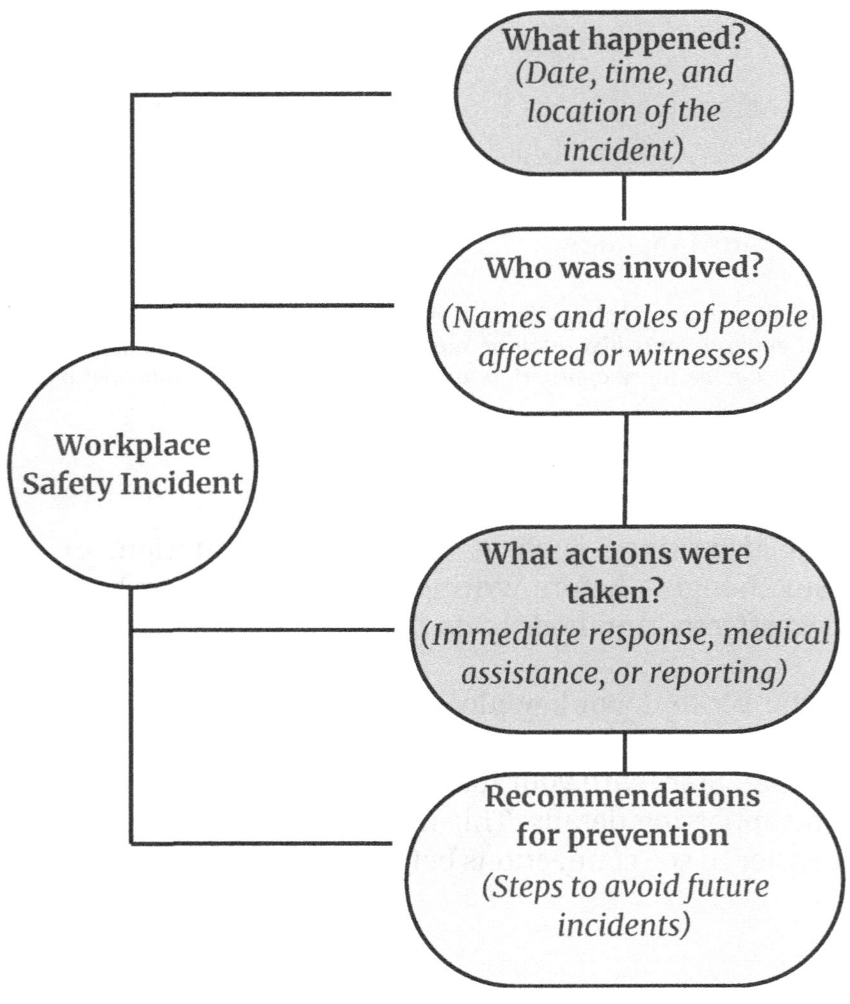

- **Example of a Rough Draft Workplace Safety Incident Report**

Workplace Safety Incident Report
Date: March 12, 2025
Time: 2:30 PM
Location: Stockroom, ABC Supermarket

Incident Description
On March 12, 2025, at approximately 2:30 PM, an accident occurred in the stockroom of ABC Supermarket. Employee John Doe, a stock associate, slipped and fell while carrying a box of canned goods. The floor was wet due to a leak from a refrigeration unit that had not been cleaned up. John landed on his left arm and complained of pain.

Individuals Involved
- Injured Employee: John Doe (Stock Associate)
- Witnesses: Jane Smith (Cashier), Mark Brown (Supervisor)

Actions Taken

Immediately after the fall, Mark Brown, the supervisor on duty, assisted John Doe and assessed his condition. Since John reported pain in his arm, emergency medical services were called. A store first-aid kit was used to provide initial care while waiting for paramedics. Paramedics arrived at 2:50 PM and transported John to City Hospital for further evaluation.

The area was cordoned off, and a maintenance team was called to clean up the water spill and inspect the refrigeration unit. The store manager was notified immediately, and an incident report form was completed by the supervisor.

Recommendations for Prevention

- Regular inspections of refrigeration units to detect leaks early.
- Immediate cleanup protocols for spills in high-traffic areas.
- Clear signage to warn employees of wet floors.
- Mandatory safety training on hazard identification and response.

○ **Example of the Revised Version**

Workplace Safety Incident Report
Date: March 12, 2025
Time: 2:30 PM
Location: Stockroom, ABC Supermarket

Incident Description

At 2:30 PM, stock associate John Doe slipped in the stockroom while carrying canned goods. The floor was wet from a refrigeration leak that had not been cleaned up. John fell on his left arm and reported pain.

Individuals Involved

Injured Employee: John Doe (Stock Associate)
Witnesses: Jane Smith (Cashier), Mark Brown (Supervisor)

Actions Taken

- Supervisor Mark Brown assisted John and called paramedics.
- First aid was provided until emergency responders arrived at 2:50 PM.
- John was transported to City Hospital for further evaluation.
- Maintenance cleaned the spill, and the refrigeration unit was inspected.
- The store manager was notified, and an official incident report was filed.

Recommendations for Prevention

1. Routine checks on refrigeration units.
2. Immediate spill cleanup protocols.
3. Warning signs for wet floors.
4. Safety training on workplace hazards.

Why this Revision is More Effective

The revised version improves clarity and readability by using concise sentences, eliminating unnecessary words while preserving all key details. The structure is more visually accessible, with bullet points and spacing that make it easier to scan important information quickly. Additionally, the tone remains professional and to the point, emphasizing actions taken and solutions recommended rather than unnecessary descriptions.

Final Checklist

Before finalizing your work, use this checklist to ensure your writing is well-structured and polished:

1. Is my message clear in the first sentence?
2. Did I avoid repeating the same idea?
3. Are my main points easy to identify?
4. Did I remove unnecessary words?

Activity 63: The email below is unorganized and repetitive. Rewrite it in a clear, structured, and professional format, following the steps discussed in the lesson.

Hi, I hope you're doing well. I wanted to check if I could switch my shift with a colleague this Friday because I have a personal commitment. It's quite important, and I was wondering if this would be possible. I was thinking maybe someone could take my shift on Friday, and I could take theirs on another day. If there's any issue, please let me know. I don't want to cause problems, and I can also try to manage otherwise. Thanks a lot for your time and consideration. Looking forward to hearing from you soon.

Subject:

Body:

Dear ,

Best regards,

Activity 64: Choose one of the following writing prompts and compose a clear, concise message, applying the structure from the lesson.

Option 1: Write an email to your department manager proposing a new training session or workshop that would benefit the team. Your email should briefly explain why the training is needed, outline its key benefits, and encourage your manager to consider the idea.

Option 2: Write a customer complaint report documenting a concern raised by a client or customer. Include key details such as what the complaint was about, how it was handled, and any resolution steps taken.

Note: Model answers are provided in the answer key.

Key Points Outline

Lesson 35: Practical Everyday Writing

This lesson focuses on essential everyday writing skills, helping you express yourself clearly, professionally, and effectively in both formal and personal situations. By practicing structured writing, you will gain confidence in handling real-world communication, whether you're making a formal request, filing a complaint, reflecting on personal growth, or inquiring about important information.

Writing a Letter to an Institution

In many situations, you may need to submit a formal written request to an institution such as a bank, university, or government office. A well-structured, professional letter ensures that your request is processed efficiently and taken seriously. Whether sending a physical letter or an email, proper formatting makes your message clear, organized, and easy to read.

Key Elements of a Well-Formatted Letter:
- A professional greeting (e.g., *Dear [Recipient's Name],*)
- A clear introduction stating the purpose of the letter.
- Logically structured paragraphs that present necessary details.
- A polite closing statement.
- Consistent alignment, spacing, and font style to maintain readability.

The Structure of a Formal Request Letter:
1. **Introduction:** Clearly state the purpose of your letter in the opening sentence. Be direct and concise about what you are requesting.
2. **Main Details:** Provide the necessary background information, including relevant reference numbers, dates, and supporting details. Explain why you are making the request and attach any required documents.
3. **Conclusion:** Close the letter with your contact details and a polite expression of appreciation for their assistance.

Model Example:
Letter to a University Requesting a Name Change on a Diploma

[Your Name]
[Your Address]
[City, State, ZIP Code]
[Your Email Address]
[Your Phone Number]
[Date]

Office of the Registrar
[University Name]
[University Address]
[City, State, ZIP Code]

Subject: Request for Name Change on Diploma

Dear *[Registrar's Name or "Office of the Registrar"]*,

I am writing to formally request a name change on my diploma due to a legal name change. I graduated from *[University Name]* in *[Graduation Year]* with a degree in *[Your Degree Program]*. My diploma was issued under my previous name, *[Previous Name]*, and I would like it to be updated to reflect my new legal name, *[New Name]*.

To support this request, I have attached the required documentation, including:
- A copy of my legal name change certificate
- A copy of my current government-issued ID
- Additional forms as specified by the university's policy

Please let me know if any further information is required to process this request. I would appreciate confirmation of receipt of my request and guidance on the expected timeline for issuing the updated diploma.

Thank you for your time and assistance. Please feel free to contact me at *[Your Email Address]* or *[Your Phone Number]* if you need any additional details.

Sincerely,
[Your Name]

Writing a Complaint Letter

At some point, you may need to formally address an issue with a product or service, whether it's a faulty purchase, poor customer service, or an unfulfilled refund. A well-written complaint letter allows you to express your concerns professionally and effectively, increasing the likelihood of a positive resolution. An effective complaint letter should be clear, factual, and solution-oriented rather than emotional or confrontational.

The Structure of a Complaint Letter:
1. **Introduction**: Clearly state the problem and include key details such as the date of purchase, order number, and previous communication regarding the issue.
2. **Details of the Issue**: Explain what happened, when it occurred, and why it is unacceptable. Be factual and specific.
3. **Requested Resolution**: Specify what action you expect (e.g., refund, replacement, compensation) and set a reasonable deadline for the company to respond.
4. **Professional Closing**: Express appreciation for their prompt attention and provide your contact details for further communication.

Imagine you purchased a product from an online store, requested a refund due to an issue, but have yet to receive it despite multiple follow-ups. Your complaint letter should clearly outline the problem and request a resolution within a reasonable timeframe.

Model Example: Complaint Letter about a Delayed Refund

[Your Name]
[Your Address]
[City, State, ZIP Code]
[Your Email Address]
[Your Phone Number]
[Date]

Customer Service Department
[Retailer Name]
[Company Address]
[City, State, ZIP Code]

Subject: Urgent: Delayed Refund for Order #[Order Number]

Dear Customer Service Team,

I am writing to formally request the status of my refund for Order #*[Order Number]*, which I placed on *[Purchase Date]* through your online store. According to your refund policy, I should have received the reimbursement within *[stated timeframe]*, but as of today, I have yet to receive the amount.

I initially requested a refund on *[Date of Refund Request]*, and I followed up on *[Date of Follow-up]* but have not received a response. Given the circumstances, this delay is unacceptable, and I kindly ask that this matter be resolved as soon as possible.

I request that the refund be processed within [reasonable timeframe, e.g., five business days] to avoid further escalation. Please confirm once the refund has been issued. I appreciate your prompt attention to this matter and look forward to your response.

If you require any additional information, please feel free to contact me at *[Your Email]* or *[Your Phone Number]*.

Sincerely,
[Your Name]

Writing for Self-Reflection and Personal Growth

Personal writing is a powerful tool for organization, goal-setting and self-improvement. Structured writing - such as to do lists and personal journals - helps clarify your thoughts and keep you accountable.

Using To-Do Lists for Productivity

Successful professionals and students use structured to-do lists to manage their workload, reduce stress, and increase productivity. A well-organized list helps prioritize tasks and ensures that important work gets done on time.

Key Elements of an Effective To-Do List:
- **Use action-oriented language** (e.g., *Submit report by 5pm* instead of *Work on report*).
- **Break down** large tasks into smaller, manageable steps.
- **Prioritize** tasks based on urgency and importance.

Self-Reflection through Writing

Keeping a personal journal for self-reflection is a valuable tool for tracking progress, identifying challenges, and reflecting on your actions and resolutions. Writing regularly helps you become more intentional about personal and professional growth by assessing what has worked well and what needs improvement.

Key Elements of Self-Reflection Writing:
- **Be specific** - focus on concrete experiences and lessons learned.
- **Be honest** - acknowledge both successes and challenges.
- **Be forward-thinking** - set a plan for improvement.

 # Activity 65: Choose one of the following writing tasks and apply the key elements discussed in this lesson to structure your response effectively.

Option 1: Write a **formal request letter** to your bank requesting a replacement card for a lost or expired bank card.

Option 2: Write a **professional complaint letter** regarding an online order that was delivered damaged.

Option 3: Write a **personal reflection** about your learning experience with this book, highlighting key takeaways and areas for further improvement.

Key Points Outline

 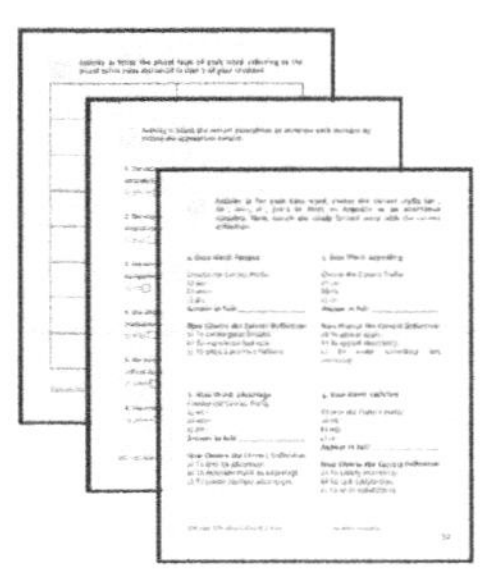

PROGRESS PORTAL 3: Reflect and Assess

Well done on completing Module 3! You've explored word origins, expanded your vocabulary, and refined your writing skills for professional and everyday communication. I hope that these lessons have equipped you with valuable tools to write with confidence and precision.

As you continue your learning journey, keep this book as a reference and revisit any lessons or vocabulary that you feel need extra practice. If you haven't already, download the supplementary worksheets for additional exercises that reinforce what you've learned in each unit.

I'd also love to hear your feedback! Your thoughts on this book will help me improve future editions and better support learners like you. It only takes under five minutes to answer three quick questions. You'll find the link and QR code to the questionnaire below.

Scan the code  or visit:
https://natashascripts.com/feedback-form

Final Test
Now, when you're ready, it's time to take the final test and celebrate your progress. You've come so far—keep going!

Take the final assessment online by scanning the QR code or visiting https://natashascripts.com/progressportals/

Password for Progress Portal 3, Assessment 3: **FinalTest8-10**

Assessment 3

Score:

____

Date:

____

Reflection

1. What concepts or skills from Units 8-10 do you feel confident about?

2. Which areas or topics do you find most challenging, and why?

3. What strategy can you use to improve in these areas?
(*E.g., review examples or practice tricky words daily.*)

Answer Key

Unit 1: Activity 1

1. Let me know when **you're** ready to discuss your next project.
2. Don't forget to bring **your** ID badge to work tomorrow.
3. Please double-check **your** email for any spelling mistakes before sending it.
4. I can tell **you're** really committed to improving your skills.
5. **You're** welcome to join us for lunch if you have time.
6. I think **your** lunch is in the fridge, right next to mine.
7. **Your** appointment with the manager is scheduled for 3 p.m.
8. If **you're** planning to take a vacation, be sure to submit your request early.
9. **You're** doing a great job with those customer orders—keep it up!
10. Remember to lock **your** car before coming inside.
11. Whether **you're** exploring a new city or revisiting old memories, travel always broadens **your** perspective.
12. Trust in **your** abilities, even when **you're** unsure of the outcome.
13. Whether **you're** meeting new people or deepening connections, **your** communication skills are key.
14. When **you're** facing new challenges, remember that **your** resilience is one of your greatest assets.
15. **Your** determination shows, even when **you're** faced with setbacks.

Unit 1: Activity 2

1. The company is proud of **its** commitment to reducing waste and improving sustainability.
2. The tree lost many of **its** leaves during the strong winds last night.
3. The microwave keeps beeping to let me know **it's** done heating up my lunch.
4. A cat uses **its** tail to help maintain balance when climbing.
5. The carwash is busy today, but **it's** worth the wait to get a spotless vehicle.
6. **It's** been a long day, so I think I'll relax with a cup of tea when I get home.
7. The smartphone has a crack on **its** screen, so I'll need to get it repaired.
8. The restaurant is known for **its** cozy atmosphere and friendly service.
9. **It's** a good idea to check your grocery list before heading to the supermarket.
10. At the coffee shop, **it's** best to order early to avoid the morning rush.
11. The dog chased its tail for hours, never seeming to get tired.

Unit 1: Activity 2 continued

12. It's been a long time since we last had a family gathering.
13. Its small size makes the hummingbird one of the most fascinating creatures in the animal kingdom.

Unit 1: Activity 3

1. During the Renaissance, **there** was a surge in art, literature, and scientific discovery.
2. The students presented **their** research on how climate change affects local wildlife.
3. Historians study the lives of individuals to understand **their** impact on society.
4. **They're** launching a new art exhibit downtown to celebrate local artists.
5. At the library, **they're** hosting workshops on digital skills for adults.
6. **They're** remembering loved ones who served in the military on Veterans Day.
7. In the library, **there** are countless resources on global cultures and traditions.
8. **There** was a significant shift in society when the internet became widely accessible.
9. Parents are concerned about **their** children's safety on social media.
10. Artists often find inspiration in **their** surroundings, from cityscapes to rural landscapes.
11. Since **they're** both teachers, they often discuss educational trends and challenges.
12. If you walk down Main Street, **there** are several small businesses worth exploring.
13. In the library, **there** are countless resources on global cultures and traditions.
14. Many people take pride in **their** cultural heritage and celebrate it through festivals.
15. **There** is a museum in town that showcases the history of the early settlers.

Unit 1: Activity 4

1. Studies show that individuals who engage in active learning retain information better **than** those who passively read or listen. This is why techniques like summarizing, questioning, and self-testing are encouraged, as they involve deeper cognitive processing than simple memorization.

2. In statistical analysis, larger sample sizes generally provide more accurate results **than** smaller ones. With more data points, researchers can reduce the margin of error and increase the reliability of their findings.

SPELLING FOR ADULTS ©2025

Unit 1: Activity 4 (continued)

3. In a controlled experiment, scientists observe and record data to test a hypothesis. First, they set up the experiment by identifying variables and constants. Then, they run multiple trials, carefully noting results. Afterward, they analyze the data to see if it supports or disproves their original hypothesis.

4. Some areas receive significantly more rainfall **than** others, leading to diverse ecosystems around the world. For example, rainforests experience high levels of precipitation, creating lush environments, whereas deserts receive less rain, resulting in arid landscapes with specialized plant and animal life.

5. In many novels, the climax represents a turning point for the protagonist. The character might face a dilemma or make a crucial decision. **Then**, in the resolution, the consequences of that decision are revealed, bringing the story to a conclusion and leaving readers with a lasting impression.

6. The Impressionist movement began with a small group of artists who challenged traditional painting techniques. **Then**, as their work gained recognition, more artists adopted the style, leading to broader acceptance of Impressionism.

7. In physics, it's often said that actions have consequences. For instance, friction is stronger on rough surfaces **than** on smooth ones, causing more resistance to motion.

8. In the animal kingdom, some species are more adaptable to changing environments **than** others. Animals with greater genetic diversity often have a better chance of surviving in fluctuating conditions. This adaptability explains why certain species thrive in various habitats while others are confined to specific regions.

9. The Industrial Revolution marked a period of intense change in production and technology. Before this era, most manufacturing was done by hand. **Then**, with the invention of machinery, factory production soared, leading to a rapid expansion of cities as people moved closer to factories for work.

10. To solve a complex equation, you begin by isolating one variable. **Then**, you simplify each term step-by-step until you reach a solution. Once the solution is found, it's important to double-check each step to ensure the calculations were correct.

Unit 1: Activity 5

1. In medieval times, knights would **wear** heavy armor to protect themselves in battle.
2. True peace is often found **where** silence meets the soul.
3. The tools **were** scattered across the workbench, ready for the next repair.
4. Doctors and nurses **wear** scrubs to maintain hygiene and comfort during their shifts.
5. **We're** determined to finish the project on time, despite the setbacks.
6. Communities thrive **where** people feel safe and supported.
7. The café **where** we had breakfast had the best view of the mountains.
8. We **were** discussing next quarter's goals when the fire alarm went off.
9. The vegetables **were** overcooked, but the sauce saved the dish.
10. **We're** lucky to live in an era where technology connects us so easily.
11. Legends say that warriors would **wear** talismans to protect them from evil spirits.
12. He prefers to **wear** casual clothes, even when attending formal events.
13. The workers **were** trained on the new assembly line procedures last week.
14. **Where** the road forks, you'll find a hidden trail leading to the beach.
15. I'll show you **where** I found the recipe for this delicious cake.
16. While hiking up the trail, **we're** hoping to catch a glimpse of the sunrise.
17. **We're** planning a surprise birthday party, so don't let the secret slip!
18. Customers **were** lining up outside the store for the grand opening.
19. In traditional Japanese culture, women **wear** kimonos during formal ceremonies.
20. In the kitchen, **we're** experimenting with new spices to create a unique dish.

Unit 1: Activity 6

1. It took me **two** tries **to** parallel park, but in my defense, the space was tiny.
2. The spicy curry was delicious, but it was way **too** hot for my taste buds **to** handle!
3. I went **to** the gym this morning... only **to** sit in the café and drink coffee.
4. She went **to** the store **to** buy milk but came back with a new coffee machine instead.
5. The kids tried **to** sneak **to** the fridge at midnight,

Unit 1: Activity 6 (continued)

6. She said she'd bring snacks **to** the party **too**, but all she brought was a bag of ice.

7. He works **too** hard during the week and then naps **too** much on the weekends.

8. She brought **two** cakes **to** the office party - one to share and one **to** hide in her desk.

9. I set my alarm **two** hours early, but somehow, I was still late for work.

10. I drove to the meeting an hour early, only **to** realize it was scheduled for tomorrow.

11. He wanted **to** ask for a raise, but his nerves got the best of him—so he asked for a stapler instead.

12. I wanted **to** join the dance class **too**, but my two left feet had other plans.

13. The puppy was **too** cute **to** resist, so now I'm a proud dog mom of three.

14. I asked for **two** sugars in my coffee, and the barista handed me **two** cookies instead.

15. The magician said he had **two** tricks up his sleeve, but all I saw was a rabbit and a pigeon.

Unit 1: Activity 7

1. She walked **by** the shop, tempted to **buy** the dress in the window, but instead whispered **bye** to her reflection.

2. The library is located right **by** the main square in town.

3. The parcel was delivered **by** courier within two days.

4. If you **buy** three books, you get a discount on the fourth one.

5. She waved **bye** to her friends as the train pulled out of the station.

6. "**Bye** for now!" she said, promising to call later that evening.

7. I stopped **by** the bakery to **buy** a loaf of bread and said **bye** to the friendly cashier.

8. He saved enough money to finally **buy** his dream car.

9. There's a beautiful café **by** the lake where you can enjoy the view.

10. "Say **bye** to Grandma before we leave," Mom reminded her kids.

11. The little girl cheerfully said **bye** to her teacher on the last day of school.

12. I need to **buy** some groceries before the store closes.

13. He completed the project **by** working late every night.

14. On my way **by** the park, I decided to **buy** an ice cream and waved **bye** to a friend.

15. You can **buy** tickets online or swing **by** the box office to pick them up in person.

16. "I'll stop **by** your house tomorrow to say **bye** before my trip," he promised.

17. She said **bye** to her friends as they walked **by** the coffee shop.

18. They hurried **by** the ticket counter to **buy** their passes and whispered a quick **bye** to the attendant.

Unit 1: Activity 8

1. It's nice to finally be **here** after such a long journey.

2. Stand **here** for a moment, and I'll be back with the paperwork.

3. I can't believe it's already been a year since we moved **here**.

4. You should **hear** the advice of those who have more experience in this field.

5. I often **hear** my favorite song playing in my head, even when there's no music around.

6. The instructions say to click **here** to complete your registration.

7. He strained to **hear** what the speaker was saying over the chatter in the crowd.

8. It's so quiet in this library that you can **hear** a pin drop.

9. Please place your bags **here** by the door so we can keep the area clear.

10. It's great to see everyone gathered **here** for the family reunion.

11. She loves to **hear** the sound of waves crashing on the shore during her morning walks.

12. I could **hear** the birds chirping outside my window as the sun rose.

13. The best coffee shop in town is right **here** on this corner.

14. I can't wait to **hear** your thoughts on the new book I recommended.

15. Did you **hear** the thunder last night during the storm?

16. Let's sit **here** and enjoy the sunset together.

17. **Here** in the park, you can often **hear** the cheerful laughter of children playing.

18. I love it **here** by the ocean because I can **hear** the soothing sound of the waves.

Unit 1: Activity 9

1. The color **of** the sky changed as the sun set.

2. She was proud **of** her accomplishments.

3. The bird flew **off** the branch when it heard a noise.

4. She carefully took her coat **off** before hanging it up.

5. The book **of** poems was a bestseller.

6. The alarm clock went **off** at exactly 6 a.m.

7. The scent **of** fresh flowers filled the room.

8. He jumped **off** the diving board into the pool.

9. Please wipe the dust **off** the shelf before arranging the books.

10. He's a man **of** great wisdom and kindness.

11. The idea **of** traveling to Europe excites her.

12. The sale offers 20% **off** all electronics this weekend.

Unit 1: Activity 9 (continued)

13. Turn the television **off** if no one is watching.
14. A piece **of** cake would be perfect for dessert.
15. The crown **of** the king was adorned with precious jewels.
16. The power went **off** during the thunderstorm.
17. The aroma **of** freshly baked bread filled the kitchen.
18. A bouquet **of** roses was placed on the dining table.
19. He brushed **off** the crumbs from his shirt after lunch.
20. The car sped **off** as soon as the traffic light turned green.

Unit 1: Activity 10

1. Can you **write** a brief summary of the book for the class?
2. You were absolutely **right** about the movie being fantastic!
3. Turn **right** at the next stoplight, and you'll see the bookshop.
4. It's important to do the **right** thing, even when no one is watching.
5. He likes to **write** poetry in his free time to relax.
6. She decided to **write** her memoirs as a gift for her grandchildren.
7. She has every **right** to express her opinion during the discussion.
8. The repairman fixed the issue and got the machine working **right** again.
9. If you don't **write** regularly, your handwriting may become less legible.
10. He stood up for what he believed was **right**.
11. During the meeting, I was asked to **write** the minutes for everyone.
12. The beach is just a short walk to the **right** of the hotel entrance.
13. After the argument, she called to make things **right** with her friend.
14. If you **write** down your goals, you're more likely to achieve them.
15. He asked me to **write** a recommendation letter for his job application.
16. I checked the map twice, and we're heading in the **right** direction.
17. The **right** tool for the job can make all the difference in how quickly it's done.
18. You should **write** a thank-you note to show your appreciation.
19. They hired a journalist to **write** an article about the upcoming event.
20. She plans to **write** a novel about her travels around the world.

Unit 2: Activity 11

1. Nouns ending in a silent "e" usually end in "-es" in the plural, e.g. *cue   cues*. **TRUE**
2. Most nouns ending with a consonant generally form their plural by adding the suffix "-s." **TRUE**
3. Nouns ending in the hissing sounds "ss," "z," and "x" usually form their plural by simply adding "s." **FALSE**
4. A singular noun ending in a vowel followed by a "y," such as "donkey," usually forms its plural by adding the suffix "-s." **TRUE**
5. The swishing sounds in singular nouns are those ending in "-sh" or "-ch." **TRUE**
6. Most nouns ending in "-is," such as "analysis," form their plural by replacing the suffix with "-es." **TRUE**
7. The plural of "monkey" is "monkies." **FALSE**
8. Most nouns ending in "-ff" form their plural by adding the suffix "-es," as in *cliff   cliffes*. **FALSE**
9. Nouns such as "bench," "class," and "box" form their plurals by adding the suffix "-es." **TRUE**
10. The plural of "roof" is "rooves." **FALSE**
11. "Thesis," "basis," and "emphasis," change to "theses," "bases," and "emphases," in their plural forms. **TRUE**
12. "Axe" becomes "axes" in its plural form, whereas "axis" also becomes "axes" in its plural form (different meaning). **TRUE**
13. "Chair" becomes "chaires," while "Church" becomes "churchs" in their plural forms. **FALSE**
14. "Dress" becomes "dresses," while "address" becomes "addresses" in their plural forms. **TRUE**
15. "Match" becomes "matches," while "stomach" becomes "stomachs" in their plural form. **TRUE**

Unit 2: Activity 12

Administrators	Brushes
Sales	Families
Benches	Knives
Cashiers	Selves
Calves	Copies
Factories	Tasks
Nurses	Services
Lives	Electricians
Enemies	Plumbers
Dishes	Watches
Classes	Buzzes
Taxes	Orders
Supplies	Boxes
Drawers	Stores
Barcodes	Handcuffs
Badges	Churches
Wives	Wolves
Chiefs	Roofs
Halves	Scarfs/Scarves

Unit 2: Activity 13

1. The musicians set up their **drums** on stage, ready to kick off the evening concert.
2. The bakers placed the freshly baked **loaves** on the counter.
3. The artist painted vivid scenes of bustling **cities**.
4. The data were plotted along the X and Y **axes**.
5. The farmer tended to his cattle, including the newborn **calves**.
6. The author's new book explores ancient myths and modern **mysteries**.
7. The museum showcased ancient **artifacts** from various civilizations.
8. The software consists of multiple **frameworks** that interact seamlessly.
9. **Countries** from neighboring nations joined to discuss trade agreements.
10. The office was filled with neatly organized **desks**, each equipped with a computer and a stack of files.
11. The thieves were caught after stealing priceless **knives**.
12. They organized several fun **activities** for the children at the party.
13. During the parade, colorful **flags** representing different states were carried by the participants.
14. The **elves** in the story helped the shoemaker make elegant shoes.
15. The teacher ignored the **scoffs** from the students as she announced the surprise quiz.
16. The new software will streamline our **processes**.
17. Researchers presented their **analyses** at the conference.
18. The jury listened to all the **witnesses**.
19. Painters cleaned their **brushes** after finishing the mural.
20. The community organized events at local **churches**.
21. The teacher prepared challenging **quizzes** for the students.
22. They collected antique pocket **watches**.
23. The new law introduces higher **taxes**.
24. The **wolves** howled in the distance under the full moon.

Unit 2: Activity 14

1. The **cat's** are playing with their toys. **INCORRECT - CATS**

2. The **student's** attended the assembly in the auditorium. **INCORRECT - STUDENTS**

3. The **teachers** discussed their plans for the upcoming semester. **CORRECT**

4. The **car's** in the parking lot need washing. **INCORRECT - CARS**

5. The **chair's** in the conference room are brand new. **INCORRECT - CHAIRS**

Unit 2: Activity 14 (continued)

6. The **dogs** were barking loudly in the park. **CORRECT**

7. The **flowers** in the garden bloom every spring. **CORRECT**

8. The **company's** were presenting their new ideas at the expo. **INCORRECT - COMPANIES**

9. The **players** celebrated their victory after the match. **CORRECT**

10. The **cake's** at the bakery looked delicious. **INCORRECT - CAKES**

11. The **phone's** on the desk need to be charged. **INCORRECT - PHONES**

12. The **tree's** in the orchard are full of ripe fruit. **INCORRECT - TREES**

13. The **hotel's** in the city were fully booked for the event. **INCORRECT - HOTELS**

14. The **offices** were closed for the holiday weekend. **CORRECT**

Unit 3: Activity 16

How to Be a Successful Professional in Today's Workplace

Starting a new job can feel **awkward** at the beginning, but with the right mindset and strategies, you can **acquire** the skills and confidence needed to excel. It's **necessary** to **acknowledge** your own strengths and areas for improvement, as well as to **believe** in your potential for growth.

One critical skill is time management, so keeping a well-organized **calendar** is a must. Being punctual and prepared shows your **colleagues** that you value their time. Additionally, clear **judgment** and the ability to **foresee** potential challenges are key to making **successful** decisions in the workplace.

Maintaining professionalism also requires staying **conscious** of your actions and their impact on others. A strong **conscience** will guide you in treating others with respect and integrity. Avoid the temptation to **exaggerate** achievements; honesty will earn you lasting trust.

Unit 3: Activity 16 (continued)

If you're unsure about a decision, it's always wise to seek advice. Experts often **recommend** consulting trusted mentors or colleagues. Don't be afraid to ask for help—it's not a sign of weakness but a step toward improvement.

Mistakes are part of the journey, and learning to take responsibility for them shows maturity and resilience. Owning up to a missed deadline or clarifying a misunderstanding directly will earn you respect and demonstrate maturity.

By following these principles, you'll **definitely** set yourself on the path to success, both personally and professionally.

Unit 3: Activity 17

1. D. sep**ara**te
2. B. emb**arra**ss
3. C. ab**sen**ce
4. D. d**esper**ate
5. A. bel**ie**ve

Unit 4: Activity 19

1. The speaker's rapid delivery and heavy accent rendered his presentation almost **unintelligible** to the audience.
2. Depending on **unreliable** public transportation often made her late for work.
3. The renowned artist was so private and **unapproachable** that even his closest colleagues rarely saw his work in progress.
4. It was **unusual** to see snow in April, even for a region known for its unpredictable weather.
5. Visiting the ancient ruins of Machu Picchu was an **unforgettable** experience that left the travelers in awe.
6. Many environmental issues remain **unaddressed**, despite growing evidence of their impact on global health.
7. The **unpredictable** weather in the mountains made planning the hike a challenge.
8. For centuries, the idea of human flight seemed **unattainable**, until the Wright brothers achieved it in 1903.
9. The restoration of the historic painting was so seamless that the repairs were **unnoticeable** even to art experts.
10. The **unbelievable** resilience of people during natural disasters often becomes a source of global inspiration.
11. The outdated design of the office space was so **unappealing** that employees avoided using the break room entirely.
12. Despite multiple attempts, their efforts to reach a compromise remained **unsuccessful**.

Unit 4: Activity 19 (continued)

13. The sudden and **uncontrollable** laughter of the audience turned the serious lecture into a comedic event.
14. The company's rapid growth led to an **unmanageable** workload for its under-resourced teams.
15. The heated argument over seating arrangements felt entirely **unnecessary** during such an important meeting.
16. The eerie silence in the abandoned house was deeply **unsettling** to the group of explorers.
17. Her leadership during the crisis was **unparalleled**, setting a standard for others to follow.
18. His **unquestionable** dedication to the project earned him the admiration of his peers.
19. Advances in artificial intelligence have opened doors to **unimaginable** possibilities in medicine and technology.
20. The manager apologized profusely when the requested files were **unavailable** due to a system crash.

Unit 4: Activity 21

1. Her manager seemed to **disapprove** of the casual tone she used in the formal email.
2. The team felt **disheartened** after their hard work on the project went unnoticed during the presentation.
3. Many customers were **dissatisfied** with the product's quality, leaving critical reviews online.
4. In the 19th century, women faced significant **disadvantages** in accessing education and professional opportunities.
5. The gallery's **disorganized** layout made it difficult for visitors to fully appreciate the artwork on display.
6. Due to declining sales, the company decided to **discontinue** its line of luxury notebooks.
7. The scientist's groundbreaking discovery was met with **disbelief** until further experiments confirmed the results.
8. His **disregard** for safety protocols led to an accident on the construction site.
9. The artist's unconventional style was initially deemed **disagreeable** by critics, only to be celebrated decades later.
10. The politician's **dishonest** claims were quickly debunked by investigative journalists.
11. In high-stress situations, it's important to **disengage** from heated arguments to maintain professionalism.
12. The mechanic had to **disassemble** the engine to identify the source of the unusual noise.

Unit 4: Activity 23

1. Her **misguided** attempt to solve the problem only made the situation more complicated for everyone involved.

2. Vincent van Gogh's art was largely **misunderstood** during his lifetime but is celebrated today for its genius.

3. The architect realized the beams were **misaligned**, causing structural concerns in the historic building.

4. It's easy to **misjudge** someone's intentions when you're relying solely on text messages without context.

5. The employee was dismissed for repeated **misconduct**, which disrupted the office environment.

6. If you **misspell** key terms in your resume, it could give employers the wrong impression about your attention to detail.

7. The spread of **misinformation** on social media contributed to confusion about the event's start time.

8. The CEO **mismanaged** the corporation's funds, diverting them to risky investments and leaving the company in a precarious financial situation.

9. A **miscalculation** in the budget left the museum project short on funds, delaying the exhibit's opening.

10. The scientist was criticized for attempting to **misuse** the data to support a flawed hypothesis.

11. The **misfortune** of a sudden engine failure forced the pilot to make an emergency landing.

12. The email was so brief that it was easy to **misinterpret** the tone as rude instead of urgent.

13. The flashy advertisement was designed to **mislead** consumers into thinking the product was a miracle cure.

14. The lawyer warned her client not to **misrepresent** the facts during the negotiation, as it could backfire in court.

Unit 4: Activity 26

1. The documentary allowed viewers to **relive** the pivotal moments of the civil rights movement.

2. A solid understanding of art history is a **prerequisite** for enrolling in the advanced curatorial course.

3. The library decided to **reorganize** its collection by genre to improve accessibility for readers.

4. The bank agreed to **preapprove** his mortgage application, saving him time when house hunting.

5. The playwright had to **rewrite** the ending after early feedback from the test audience.

6. As a **precaution**, the museum installed climate control systems to preserve the ancient artifacts.

7. The annual reunion was the perfect opportunity to **reconnect** with former colleagues.

8. The editor invited the team to **preview** the final layout of the magazine before publication.

Unit 4: Activity 26

9. After ten years in the city, they decided to **relocate** to a quieter rural area.

10. His prior commitments will **preclude** him from attending the conference next week.

11. They decided to **prearrange** the seating for the gallery opening to ensure a smooth event.

12. After the unexpected delays, the project team decided to **reevaluate** their timeline and priorities.

13. He took extra time to **revise** his proposal before submitting it to the grant committee.

14. The IT department will **preload** the software onto all new employee laptops.

15. She stopped at the café to **refill** her thermos before heading to the office.

16. The engineering firm conducted a **pretest** of the materials to ensure safety standards were met.

17. The artist used her travels to **renew** her creative inspiration for the upcoming exhibit.

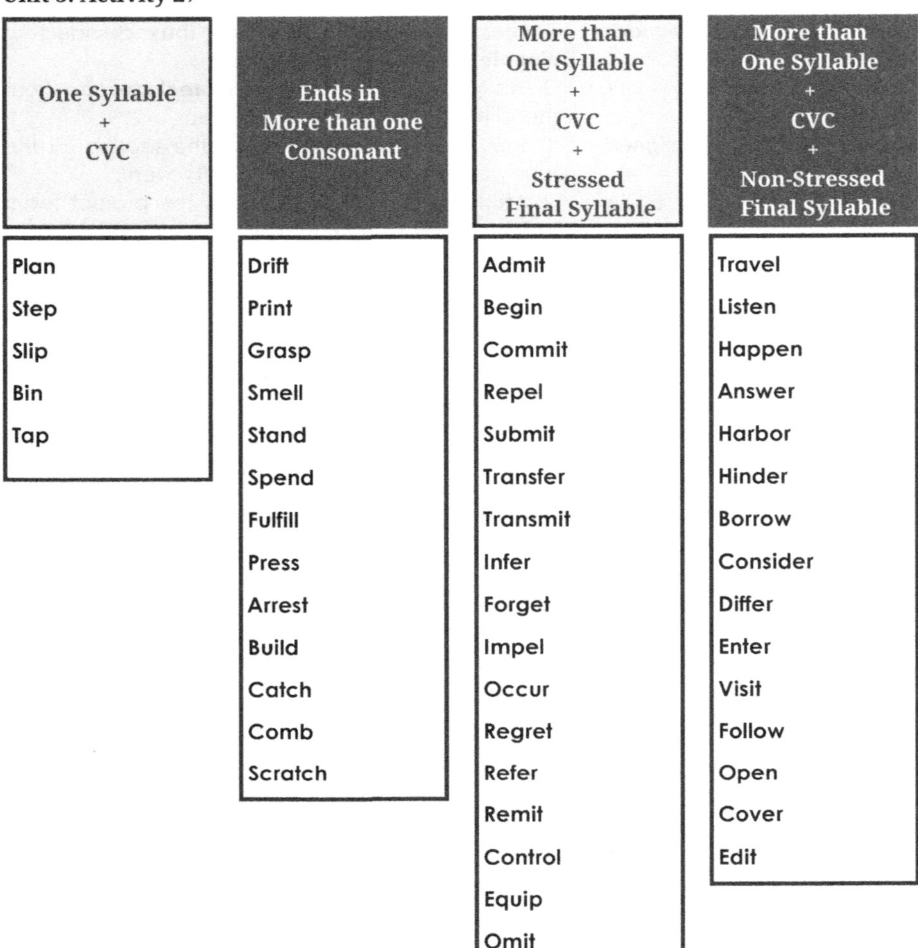

One Syllable + CVC	Ends in More than one Consonant	More than One Syllable + CVC + Stressed Final Syllable	More than One Syllable + CVC + Non-Stressed Final Syllable
Plan	Drift	Admit	Travel
Step	Print	Begin	Listen
Slip	Grasp	Commit	Happen
Bin	Smell	Repel	Answer
Tap	Stand	Submit	Harbor
	Spend	Transfer	Hinder
	Fulfill	Transmit	Borrow
	Press	Infer	Consider
	Arrest	Forget	Differ
	Build	Impel	Enter
	Catch	Occur	Visit
	Comb	Regret	Follow
	Scratch	Refer	Open
		Remit	Cover
		Control	Edit
		Equip	
		Omit	

Unit 5: Activity 28

Subject: **Follow-Up on Project Transfer and Next Steps**

Dear David,

I regret the delay in **transmitting** the revised project plan; we encountered some unforeseen challenges in finalizing the document. However, the updated files have now been **transferred** to your department for review. Please find them attached for your reference. I've also included an **edited** summary of the key points for your convenience.

Moving forward, we are considering **equipping** the team with additional resources to avoid any hindrance to the project's timeline. I recommend **following** up with the finance department regarding the **remitted** funds for the next phase. It's essential to ensure that all expenses are fully **covered** to fulfill the remaining deliverables on schedule.

If you need clarification on any aspect, feel free to refer back to the notes provided or reach out directly. I'll be **standing** by to assist with any questions or additional considerations. Thank you for your patience and continued support in ensuring the success of this project.

Best regards,
Claire

Unit 5: Activity 29

1. After **spending** weeks on the project, we **regretted** not considering all the potential challenges that could hinder our progress. By **omitting** key details in the initial report, we inadvertently delayed the **transmitting** of critical information to stakeholders. Moving forward, we are **pressing** for stricter timelines and **controlling** resources more effectively to fulfill the remaining objectives without further setbacks.

2. During the 19th century, several nations **developed** innovative cartographic techniques, which greatly improved the accuracy of **mapping** uncharted territories. Explorers often **suffered** hardships as they **entered** harsh climates to gather data, yet their perseverance **fulfilled** humanity's thirst for knowledge.

3. After **beginning** his journey as an amateur photographer, Tyler quickly found himself **committing** more time and energy to the craft. What started as a hobby soon **propelled** him into a world of creativity and discovery. On weekends, he could often be found **traveling** to scenic locations, camera in hand, **listening** to the sounds of nature while carefully **planning** his next shot. The unpredictability of capturing the perfect moment often **slipped** through his grasp, but he never gave up. Instead, he **submitted** his best work to local galleries, gaining valuable feedback and recognition. Each photograph he **printed** told a story. The results were truly worth the effort, as his portfolio became a visual diary of his artistic growth.

4. Jessica **committed** herself to a new routine of morning exercise to improve her health. Each day, she began with a series of stretches before **stepping** onto the treadmill. Gradually, she managed to increase her endurance, **propelled** by her determination to meet her fitness goals. The schedule was carefully **planned**, with rest days to allow her body to recover. Occasionally, she **slipped** on maintaining consistency, but her perseverance kept her on track. By the end of the month, she felt accomplished, having **admitted** that her hard work was starting to pay off.

Unit 5: Activity 30

1. In their latest project, the team **collaborated** effectively to achieve their goals. Each member **contributed** unique insights, while the leader **delegated** tasks strategically to ensure smooth progress. They **communicated** openly during meetings, which **facilitated** better understanding and **integrated** everyone's efforts. By the end, they **concluded** the project successfully, with results that **demonstrated** their collective strength and commitment.

Unit 5: Activity 30 continued

2. **Moving** to a new workplace can be **challenging**, but collaborating with supportive colleagues makes the transition smoother. By **communicating** openly and participating actively in team projects, employees can quickly establish rapport. **Integrating** into a new environment often requires adapting to existing workflows while **contributing** fresh ideas. With time, these efforts result in **elevating** both individual confidence and team performance.

3. The university professor **educated** her students on critical thinking skills by **encouraging** them to debate various perspectives. She **demonstrated** the value of evidence-based arguments and **illustrated** key concepts with real-world examples. Her methods **generated** enthusiasm for learning and formulated an **engaging** environment that **elevated** the students' understanding.

4. A local nonprofit has been **educating** the community about sustainability by **illustrating** its importance through interactive workshops. By demonstrating eco-friendly practices and **organizing** cleanup events, they are actively **contributing** to environmental awareness. Volunteers are participating in various initiatives, **motivated** by the belief that small actions can lead to significant change over time.

5. The debate team moved through the regional rounds with confidence, **hoping** to secure their spot at the national finals. They **analyzed** their opponents' arguments, calculating the strengths and weaknesses of each point. By **collaborating** during their preparation and **communicating** effectively on stage, they **demonstrated** a mastery of critical thinking and persuasion. As the final debate ended, they **concluded** their presentation with a powerful statement, **contributing** to a well-earned victory.

Unit 5: Activity 31

The council **agreed** to lift the village's curfew. To mark the momentous occasion, it was **decreed** that a grand festival would be held, a celebration **guaranteed** to restore hope and unity among the villagers. As the preparations unfolded, children delighted in **tiptoeing** past the dyers, **eyeing** the vibrant pigments as they worked to create colorful banners and garments. Meanwhile, a team of adventurers set out on a **canoeing** journey to the distant waterfall, to fetch rare flowers to decorate the festival grounds.

Unit 5: Activity 32

Applied	Diversified	Relayed
Betrayed	Employed	(Said)
(Bought)	Enjoyed	Simplified
Clarified	Exemplified	Spayed
Classified	Falsified	Spied
Complied	Glorified	Stayed
Conveyed	Identified	Surveyed
Decayed	Justified	Swayed
Declassified	Notified	Tried
Defied	Obeyed	Verified
Delayed	Pacified	Worried
Denied	(Paid)	
Deployed	Played	
Displayed	Portrayed	
Disqualified	Prayed	
	Purveyed	
	Quantified	
	Queried	

Unit 5: Activity 33

Managing Personal Finances

Managing finances can feel overwhelming, especially when you're **juggling** multiple expenses, investments, and unexpected costs. However, **simplifying** your financial plan can help you stay **organized** and make smarter decisions. Here are some steps to consider, using real-life scenarios to illustrate how they work.

Step 1: Classify Your Expenses

Start by **classifying** your expenses into categories like housing, utilities, groceries, and discretionary **spending**. By doing so, you'll clearly see where your money is going. For example, Samantha, a single mother, recently **identified** that 30% of her income was spent on dining out. By **quantifying** her spending habits, she was able to cut back and save for her daughter's college fund.

Step 2: Deploy a Budget

Once you've sorted your expenses, the next step is **deploying** a budget. Samantha used a budgeting app that **notified** her every time she approached her monthly limit in any category. Sticking to her plan required discipline, but the regular updates kept her accountable.

Unit 5: Activity 33 continued 1.

Step 3: Diversify Your Investments

Financial experts often recommend **diversifying** your investments to minimize risk. While Samantha focused on **paying** off debt, her brother, Brandon, was trying to grow his wealth. He began by **staying** conservative with bonds before applying some funds toward stocks. When the stock market took a downturn, his **diversified** portfolio helped him avoid significant losses.

Step 4: Pay Off Debt Strategically

Debt can feel insurmountable, but **repaying** it strategically is key. For instance, many people struggle with credit card balances, which accumulate high interest over time. By **identifying** the card with the highest interest rate and applying extra payments toward that balance, you can save money in the long run.

Samantha, for example, tackled her debts one at a time, **justifying** each payment as an investment in her future peace of mind.

Step 5: Relay Information to Family

Financial **planning** often involves others, especially family members. Samantha realized she **needed** to relay her plans to her teenage son to teach him about budgeting early. This step exemplified her dedication to **fostering** financial literacy within her household.

Step 6: Stay Vigilant Against Fraud

Another critical aspect of **managing** finances is staying alert for fraud. Scammers often use tactics like **falsifying** emails or spying on financial transactions to steal information. Samantha, for instance, received a suspicious email that **portrayed** itself as her bank. By verifying the sender's details with the bank directly, she avoided falling victim to a phishing scam.

Step 7: Enjoy Financial Freedom

Once you've taken control of your finances, it's important to pause and reflect on your progress. Samantha eventually reached a point where she could save for vacations and other luxuries, fully **enjoying** the rewards of her hard work. She even treated herself to a weekend getaway, using money she had intentionally set aside for relaxation.

Concluding Thoughts

Financial health requires effort, but by **following** these steps, you can pacify the stress and take control of your future. Whether it's through classifying, budgeting, or **staying** vigilant, small actions can lead to significant results.

Unit 6: Activity 34

Your answer may vary.

1. An **abductor** is someone who kidnaps or takes a person away illegally, which is why it is often linked to criminal acts.

2. A **contractor** might be hired to manage construction or renovation projects, such as building a house or remodeling a kitchen.

3. A **constrictor** is a type of snake that captures its prey by coiling around it and squeezing tightly until the prey cannot breathe.

4. A color **corrector** is a tool or product used to adjust or enhance colors in images, videos, or makeup, ensuring they appear balanced and visually appealing.

5. A **director** is responsible for overseeing and guiding projects or operations. They might work in creative fields, such as directing movies or theater productions, or in business, where they manage teams and organizational goals.

6. An **extractor** removes substances or materials, such as extracting juice from fruit or oil from plants.

7. An **instructor** teaches skills or knowledge to others, often in a structured environment. They might work in fields such as education, fitness, driving, or corporate training.

Unit 6: Activity 35

Examine   Examiner
Contract   Contractor
Beg   Beggar
Supervise   Supervisor
Agitate   Agitator
Instruct   Instructor
Protest   Protester

Correct   Corrector
Receive   Receiver
Format   Formatter
Accelerate   Accelerator
Sketch   Sketcher
Propel   Propeller
Log   Logger

Unit 6: Activity 35 continued

Transgress   Transgressor
Educate   Educator
Inhibit   Inhibitor
Advise   Adviser
Program   Programmer
Process   Processor
Research   Researcher
Modulate   Modulator
Audit   Auditor
Adapt   Adapter

Oppress   Oppressor
Spell   Speller
Quit   Quitter
Travel   Traveler
Contend   Contender
Trespass   Trespasser
Distill -   Distiller
Kiss   Kisser
Obstruct   Obstructor
Incise   Incisor

Unit 6: Activity 36

1. B. adjudicator
2. A impounder
3. B. assessor
4. B. estimator
5. A. disrupter
6. A. watcher
7. B. repressor
8. A. compounder
9. B. solicitor
10. A. extinguisher
11. B. suppressor
12. B. confessor
13. B. offeror

Unit 6: Activity 37

1. A Legal Dispute: adjudicator, solicitor, offeror

2. Safety at the Factory: impounder, compounder, watcher.

3. Work on a Farm: irrigator, transporter, selector

4. Charity Gala: adopter, motivator, collector, director.

Unit 6: Activity 38

The scientist conducted **molecular** research to analyze how atoms interact at a microscopic level.

The professor emphasized the importance of using **particular** reasoning rather than jumping to conclusions.

The **circular** design of the conference hall allows for better acoustics.

The **spectacular** event attracted thousands of people and was a huge success.

The hospital specializes in treating **vascular** disorders related to blood circulation.

The telescope provided a clearer view of celestial objects, enhancing **ocular** observations.

Unlike religious schools, public education systems follow a **secular** curriculum.

The new café quickly became **popular** among students because of its relaxed atmosphere and great coffee.

Engineers designed the bridge's supports to be perfectly **perpendicular** to the ground for stability.

The **nuclear** energy plant generates power for the entire city.

Unit 6: Activity 39

1. Arranged in a straight line   Linear
2. Relating to the sun   **Solar**
3. Having a shape with three sides **Triangular**
4. Affecting the heart and blood vessels **Cardiovascular**
5. Having two opposite extremes   **Bipolar**
6. Relating to the moon   **Lunar**
7. Consisting of small particles   **Granular**
8. Relating to everyday speech or informal language   **Vernacular**
9. Referring to a structured table format **Tabular**
10. Relating to roots or nerve roots   **Radicular**

Unit 6: Activity 40 (Model Answers)
Answers may vary.

1. **Cellular** technology has made communication much faster and more accessible. At work, I rely on my cellular network to send emails, attend virtual meetings, and stay connected with my team even when I'm not in the office.

Unit 6: Activity 40 (continued)

2. Having a **granular** understanding of a project allows managers to track expenses carefully and prevent overspending. For example, in budget planning, breaking down costs into granular details helps allocate resources efficiently and avoid unnecessary expenses.

3. At my previous job, an **insular** mindset among senior staff prevented the company from adopting modern digital tools. They were unwilling to consider new approaches, which made processes inefficient and caused the company to fall behind competitors.

4. My previous job had **irregular** work shifts, which made it difficult to plan personal activities. Some weeks I worked early mornings, while other weeks I had night shifts, making it hard to maintain a regular sleep schedule.

5. One of my most **singular** achievements was delivering a speech at an international conference. It was the first time I spoke in front of such a large audience, and the experience greatly boosted my confidence.

6. During a construction project, a contractor made an error, causing **collateral** damage to the neighboring building. Although the damage was unintended, the company had to pay for repairs.

7. In a recent debate, two colleagues had **polar** opinions on remote work. One argued that working from home improves productivity, while the other insisted that in-person collaboration is essential for team success.

Unit 6: Activity 41 (Model Answers)
Answers may vary.

1. His schedule is very regular, as he starts work at 8 AM, takes lunch at noon, and finishes at exactly 5 PM every day.

2. hat face looks familiar to me, but I can't remember if I've seen him at work, on television, or at the gym.

3. The policy was unpopular among employees because it reduced their remote work days and required longer office hours.

4. She has a particular way of organizing her work, carefully labeling all documents and color-coding her files for efficiency.

5. The sunset over the mountains was spectacular, with shades of orange, pink, and purple lighting up the entire sky.

Culin______**ary**   Rudiment **ary**____   Rosem________**ary**

Advers____**ary**_   Precaution**ary**____   Sal________ **ary**

Ancill____**ary**   Prelimin__**ary**_   Sanctu______**ary**

Annivers__**ary**___   Prim____**ary**   Burgl______**ary**

Arbitr____**ary**   Pulmon__**ary**_   Complement__**ary**___

Evolution_**ary**____   Respirat__**ory**_   Brib______ **ery**

Itiner____**ary**   Regulat__**ory**_   Brew______ **ery**

Machin__**ery**_   Revis____**ory**   Brav______ **ery**

Imag____**ery**   Satisfact__**ory**_   Mock______ **ery**

Forg____**ery**   Sens____**ory**   Mast______ **ery**

Glitt____**ery**   Flow____**ery**   Adjudicat____**ory**

Fish______**ery**   Auxili____**ary**   Deliv______**ery**

Eat______**ery**   Caution__**ary**_   Recov____**ery**

Drap____**ery**   Contr____**ary**   Refin____**ery**

Brok____**ery**   Diet____**ary**   Robb____**ery**

Distill__**ery**   Extraordin **ary**___   Savag____**ery**

Reaction_**ary**_   Statut____**ory**   Collaborat_**ory**___

Salut____**ary**   Transit__**ory**_   Contribut_**ory**___

Sanit____**ary**   Interrogat_**ory**____   Conservat_**ory**__

Sug______**ary**   Investigat_**ory**___   Conciliat__**ory**__

Terti____**ary**   Invent____**ory**   Compuls__**ory**_

Derogat_**ory**_   Illus____**ory**   Anticipat__**ory**__

Depilat_**ory**   Not______**ary**   Accusat___**ory**_

Defamat_**ory**__   Secret____**ary**   Compensat**ory**___

Declarat_**ory**_   Nurs____**ery**   Audit____**ory**

Corroborat**ory**____   Perfum__**ery**_   Slav______**ery**

Scen____**ery**   Powd____**ery**   Orang____**ery**

1b) Query   9b) Recovery   17c) Accessory

2a) Rudimentary   10c) Conciliatory   18a) Centenary

3c) Arbitrary   11a) Bribery   19a) Auditory

4c) Mockery   12c) Corroboratory   20a) Auxiliary

5b) Circulatory   13b) Conservatory   21b) Ancillary

6c) Accusatory   14a) Salutary   22c) Accusatory

7a) Sanctuary   15a) Forgery   23b) Compulsory

8b) Artillery   16a) Itinerary   24c) Anticipatory

Unit 7: Activity 45

C	Hard	Soft	C	Hard	Soft
Ac**c**urate	*		Con**c**ern		*
Relu**c**tant	*		**C**ivilized		*
Voi**c**eover		*	Ac**c**entuate		*
Circuit	*		Toxi**c**ology	*	
Barri**c**ade	*		Sacrifi**c**e		*
Re**c**urring	*		**C**rypto	*	
Autocra**c**y		*	**C**arrier	*	
Tri**c**ycles		*	**C**entenary		*
Ac**c**use	*		Bra**c**kets	*	
Bureau**c**rat	*		Ex**c**eption		*
			Corporate	*	
			Academi**c**	*	

Unit 7: Activity 46

1. The CEO emphasized the importance of **corporate** responsibility, urging businesses to adopt ethical and sustainable practices.

2. The forensic scientist conducted a **toxicology** analysis to determine whether the victim had been exposed to harmful chemicals.

3. Many investors are exploring **crypto** currencies as an alternative to traditional banking systems.

4. The professor received an award for his outstanding contributions to the **academic** community, particularly in historical research.

5. Doctors must rely on **accurate** diagnostic tests to determine the best treatment for their patients.

6. Despite the pay increase, he was **reluctant** to accept the promotion due to the long working hours.

7. The ruler maintained an **autocratic** government, allowing no dissent or opposition from his advisors.

8. The athlete's **agility** and quick reflexes gave her an advantage in competitive gymnastics.

9. The company's **strategic** planning helped it survive economic downturns and stay ahead of competitors.

10. The human body takes several hours to fully **digest** a large meal, depending on the type of food consumed.

11. Good leaders **encourage** their teams by recognizing achievements and fostering a positive work environment.

12. She carries an epinephrine injector in case of a severe **allergy** to peanuts.

13. Ancient **Egyptian** hieroglyphs provide valuable insights into early civilization and religious beliefs.

14. His rude comments seemed designed to **antagonize** his opponent rather than engage in constructive debate.

15. Ignoring early warning signs can **aggravate** an existing health condition, making treatment more difficult.

16. The supervisor warned that employees who consistently **disregard** safety regulations would face disciplinary action.

17. Although digital technology dominates today, some photographers still prefer the warm tones of **analog** film cameras.

18. The novel's **epilogue** provided closure by revealing what happened to the characters years later.

19. My **colleague** and I collaborated on a research paper that was later published in an international journal.

20. After working long shifts in the hospital, the nurses experienced extreme **fatigue** and needed rest.

21. The Italian restaurant is famous for its homemade **spaghetti**, prepared using a traditional family recipe.

22. The Supreme Court **judge** ruled in favor of the plaintiff, citing a violation of constitutional rights.

23. His extensive **knowledge** of medieval history made him a sought-after lecturer at universities worldwide.

24. Scientists have developed a vaccine to combat **pathogenic** bacteria that cause life-threatening diseases.

25. The exhibit showcased **indigenous** artifacts from cultures that have inhabited the region for centuries.

1. Fring**ed**
2. Camouflag**e**able
3. Pronounc**e**ment
4. Voic**e**less
5. Danc**er**
6. Grac**e**ful
7. Trac**ing**
8. Salvag**e**able
9. Submerg**ed**
10. Outrag**e**ous
11. Enhanc**e**ment
12. Exchang**e**able
13. Voic**ing**
14. Defens**e**less
15. Juic**er**

Unit 6: Activity 48

1. The company hired an external firm to conduct an **audit** of its financial records after an internal discrepancy was discovered.
2. She decided to **augment** her skills by taking an advanced certification course in digital marketing.
3. During the police investigation, the suspect's nervous **rawness** was noted as a possible sign of deception.
4. The best-selling **author** gave an insightful talk on the process of writing compelling novels.
5. The stolen artwork was recovered and verified as **authentic** by forensic specialists.
6. After months of searching, they finally found a **lawful** house that was legally compliant with zoning laws.
7. He carefully avoided stepping on the baby, who was **crawling** on the floor.
8. The company planned to **automate** several manual processes to improve efficiency and reduce costs.
9. The famous actor was met by a large **audience** of fans at the book signing event.
10. The fugitive was declared an **outlaw** by the authorities after evading capture for years.
11. She refused to sign the contract until her **lawyer** reviewed every clause carefully.
12. The tech industry is moving toward **autonomous** systems, where machines can operate without human intervention.
13. The biggest **drawback** of working remotely is the lack of face-to-face collaboration with colleagues.
14. During the emergency, he had to **withdraw** a large sum of money from his savings account.
15. She proudly displayed the framed **autograph** of her favorite musician in her office.
16. The seafood restaurant is known for its fresh **prawn**, imported daily from the coast.

Unit 6: Activity 48 (continued)

17. The athlete's performance was so **flawless** that the judges gave her a perfect score.
18. The **auction** house sold an original painting for $2 million at last night's auction.
19. The carpenter used a **hacksaw** to cut through the thick metal pipe.
20. The pilot switched to **autopilot** mode once the plane reached cruising altitude.

Unit 6: Activity 49

Acc**ou**nt	C**ou**nselor
Am**ou**nt	C**ou**nter
Anyh**ow**	Cr**ow**n
Ar**ou**nd	Fishb**ow**l
Ar**ou**se	F**ou**nder
Ast**ou**nd	G**ow**n
Av**ow**	Homegr**ow**n
B**ou**nce	H**ow**l
B**ou**nd	J**ow**l
B**ou**t	Kn**ow**n
Breakd**ow**n	N**ow**
Br**ow**n	**Ou**tgr**ow**n
Cl**ou**d	Overthr**ow**n
Comp**ou**nd	R**ou**te
Conf**ou**nd	Spr**ou**t
C**ou**ch	St**ou**t
C**ou**ntd**ow**n	V**ou**ch

SPELLING FOR ADULTS ©2025

Unit 8: Activity 53

1.b Lose	11.b Capitol
2.a Stationary	12.b. Stationery
3.a Complement	13.b Dessert
4.b Wave	14.a Affect
5.a Principal	15.b Except
6.a Capital	16.a Desert
7.b Principle	17.a Advice
8.a Waive	18.a Accept
9.a Loose	19.b Advise
10.b Compliment	20.b Effect

Unit 8: Activity 54

1. Advise	11. Capitol
2. Advice	12. Capital
3. Effect	13. Loose
4. Affect	14. Lose
5. Accept	15. Principle
6. Except	16. Principal
7. Complement	17. Stationary
8. Compliment	18. Stationery
9. Dessert	19. Wave
10. Desert	20. Waive

Unit 8: Activity 55

1. X accept	6. X waive
2. ✓	7. X affect
3. ✓	8. ✓
4. ✓	9. ✓
5. X dessert	5. X principles

Unit 8: Activity 57
1. The Entrepreneur's Challenge

argument, government, persistent, occurrence.

Unit 8: Activity 58

1. Regular **maintenance** of machinery is essential for preventing breakdowns.
2. The **fluorescent** lights in the office made it easier to read at night.
3. Having access to higher education is a **privilege** not everyone gets.
4. Many companies are now focusing on creating a sustainable workplace for their employees.
5. The sudden storm caused **unforeseen** delays in transportation.

Unit 8: Activity 58 (continued)

6. Even after several failures, he remained **persistent** in trying to complete the project.
7. The **government** is responsible for making laws that protect citizens.
8. She felt a sense of **disappointment**/she felt **disappointed** when she didn't win the competition.
9. The team reached a **consensus** before making the final decision.
10. Drivers must have a **license** before operating a vehicle on public roads.

Unit 8: Activity 59

1. F	8. H
2. M	9. B
3. L	10. D
4. K	11. A
5. J	12. E
6. I	13. C
7. G	

Unit 9: Activity 63
Subject: Request to Swap Shift on Friday

Body:
Dear [Manager's Name],

I hope you're doing well. I am reaching out to request a shift swap on Friday, [specific date], due to a personal commitment. If possible, I can trade shifts with a colleague on another day to ensure coverage.

Please let me know if this can be arranged or if there are any concerns. I appreciate your time and consideration.

Best regards,
[Your Name]

Unit 9: Activity 64

Option 1 Model Answer

Subject: Proposal for a Team Training Session on Effective Customer Communication

Dear Ms. Andersen,

I hope you're doing well. I would like to propose a training session on Effective Customer Communication to help improve our team's ability to handle customer inquiries, resolve complaints efficiently, and enhance overall service quality.

This training would benefit our team by reducing misunderstandings with customers, improving response times, and increasing customer satisfaction ratings. Many colleagues have mentioned that they sometimes struggle with handling difficult customers, responding professionally under pressure, or maintaining a positive tone in emails and phone calls. A structured workshop led by a customer service expert could provide valuable insights and practical techniques.

Please let me know if you'd be open to discussing this further. I'd be happy to research training providers, suggest potential dates, or outline a session plan. Looking forward to your thoughts.

Best regards,
Melanie Fisher
Customer Service Representative

Unit 9: Activity 64

Option 2 Model Answer

Customer Complaint Report

Date: March 14, 2025
Customer Name: Cassandra Chessim
Location/Branch: ABC Electronics Store – Downtown Branch
Complaint Subject: Defective Laptop and Delayed Replacement

Complaint Details
Customer Cassandra Chessim reported that her Dell Inspiron 15 laptop, purchased on March 5, 2025, stopped working after two days.

She returned on March 7 and was told a replacement would arrive in one week, but as of March 14, she had received no update. Needing the laptop for work, she requested an immediate replacement or refund.

Actions Taken
- Customer service rep Jonathan Lewis confirmed her eligibility under the 14-day exchange policy.
- Store supervisor approved an immediate replacement, issuing a new Dell Inspiron 15.
- Customer received a $25 store credit as an apology for the delay.

Recommendations:
To prevent future complaints of this nature, we recommend:
- Ensure faster supplier response for replacements.
- Automate customer updates on order status.
- Offer loaner devices for extended delays.

Made in the USA
Middletown, DE
05 March 2025

72271797R00149